ARTIST TRANSCRIPTIONS PIANO

Oscar Peterson
PLAYS BROADWAY

Transcribed by Richard Tuttobene

Cover Photo Tony Russell / Redferns

ISBN-13: 978-0-634-07775-3
ISBN-10: 0-634-07775-9

HAL•LEONARD®
CORPORATION
7777 W. BLUEMOUND RD. P.O. BOX 13819 MILWAUKEE, WI 53213

Visit Hal Leonard Online at
www.halleonard.com

Oscar Peterson

BIOGRAPHY

Oscar Peterson was born August 15, 1925 in Montreal, Quebec, Canada. His parents were immigrants from the British West Indies and the Virgin Islands. His father, Daniel Peterson, was boatswain on a sailing vessel when he met Olivia John in Montreal, where she worked as a cook and housekeeper for an English family. They decided to remain in Canada, get married, and start a family.

Oscar was the fourth of five children. Originally taking an interest in the trumpet, a childhood bout of tuberculosis switched Oscar's emphasis to the piano under the tutelage of his father and later his sister, Daisy. His musical talent soon surpassed the capabilities of home teaching, and he was sent outside of the home to study. Oscar studied with the gifted Hungarian classical pianist Paul de Marky, and a warm and respectful musical friendship developed between the two.

In 1947, Oscar formed his first Canadian trio and retained this format of performance for the next several years. During this time, he remained dedicated to establishing a true trio sound. At an appearance in the Alberta Lounge in 1949, impresario Norman Granz heard him and enticed him into making a guest appearance at Carnegie Hall with his all-star concert troupe known as "Jazz at the Philharmonic." Leaving the audience awestruck, Oscar returned home for a year, then rejoined JATP as a steady member in 1950. He commenced recording with Norman Granz's Mercury label, and formed his first American duo with bassist Ray Brown.

In 1950, he was awarded the *DownBeat* Award for Best Jazz Pianist. He would go on to garner this award twelve more times during his career. He continued his extensive touring of the United States, and later, as a musical ambassador for the Canadian government, he toured Europe, Africa, South America, the Far East, and even Russia.

During these busy touring schedules, he formed a jazz school in Toronto, known as the Advanced School of Contemporary Music, which attracted students from all over the world. While on tour, he would conduct seminars and, amazingly, found time to compose his "Canadiana Suite," a salute to Canada, which was recorded with his trio and released worldwide.

Oscar has recorded with many of the jazz greats over the years. His varied albums with these giants include recordings with Louis Armstrong, Ella Fitzgerald, Count Basie, Duke Ellington, Dizzy Gillespie, Roy Eldridge, Coleman Hawkins, and Charlie Parker, but it has been the recordings with his various trios that have brought him recognition from numerous places around the world.

In recent years, Oscar has been devoting more and more time to composition. His "Hymn to Freedom" became one of the crusade hymns during the civil rights movement in the United States. He has composed music for motion pictures, including the Canadian film *Big North* for

Ontario Place in Toronto, as well as the thriller *Silent Partner*, for which he won a Genie Award in 1978. His collaboration with Norman McLaren, titled *Begone Dull Care*, won awards all over the world. Oscar also composed the soundtrack for the film *Fields of Endless Day*, which traced the Underground Railroad used by African-Americans escaping to Canada during the slavery era. In addition, he has worked with the National Film Board of Canada.

Oscar followed his motion picture work with a ballet commissioned by Les Ballets Jazz du Canada, which included a special waltz for the city of Toronto titled "City Lights." Other compositional projects included "A Suite Called Africa" and a salute to Johann Sebastian Bach's 300th birthday, written for trio and orchestra. These were followed by the "Easter Suite," which was commissioned by the BBC of London and performed with a trio on Good Friday, 1984, via nationwide television. This particular production is still broadcast annually. He also composed music for the opening ceremonies of the 1988 Calgary Winter Olympic Games. In addition to all of these, Oscar has composed over 300 other tunes, most of which have been published.

Oscar has appeared on a wide array of television productions, and has hosted his own specials where he interviewed and played with a variety of guests. His widespread appeal gave way to an unusual range in personalities that included Anthony Burgess, Andrew Lloyd Webber, Tim Rice, and Edward Heath, the former Prime Minister of England.

Oscar prefers not to use his celebrity to sway political opinions, yet he remains dedicated to the belief that his native Canada has a responsibility in leading the world in equality and justice. With this in mind, he has taken a firm stand to promote recognition and fair treatment for Canada's multi-cultural community. Because of his efforts in this field, Mr. Peterson was inducted as an Officer of the Order of Canada in 1972. He was promoted to Companion of the Order, Canada's highest civilian honor, in 1984.

In 1993, Oscar was awarded the Glenn Gould Prize. He was the third recipient of the Prize, the first with a unanimous decision, and the first ever from the realm of jazz. Over the years, Mr. Peterson has been awarded many honorary degrees, and a host of other awards, including the Praemium Imperiale (the Arts equivalent of the Nobel Prize), the UNESCO International Music Prize, the Queen's Medal, the Toronto Arts Award for Lifetime Achievement, the Governor General's Performing Arts Award, and most recently the President's Award from the International Association for Jazz Education.

Despite a mild stroke in 1993, which at first debilitated his left hand, Oscar recovered to continue his yearly pattern of worldwide concert tours, recordings, and composition.

Mr. Peterson resides in the quiet city of Mississauga, Ontario. As a citizen he insists on his privacy, which he jealously guards. His hobbies include fishing, photography and astronomy, and he is an avid audiophile and synthesist. His home contains his own private recording studio, where he can work but still be able to enjoy his family life. His passion for life, love, and music is stronger than ever.

Oscar Peterson
PLAYS BROADWAY

Oscar Peterson

DISCOGRAPHY

Blues Etude   (Limelight 818 844-2)
If I Were a Bell

Exclusively for My Friends   (Verve 314 513 830-2)
On a Clear Day (You Can See Forever)
Who Can I Turn To (When Nobody Needs Me)

The London Concert   (Pablo 2620-111-2)
People

Oscar Peterson Plays Broadway, Verve Jazz Masters 37
(Verve 314-516 893-2)
All the Things You Are
Baubles, Bangles and Beads
Body and Soul
Come Rain or Come Shine
Easter Parade
Just in Time
Strike Up the Band
The Surrey with the Fringe on Top
There's a Small Hotel
Wouldn't It Be Loverly

Oscar Peterson Plays My Fair Lady *and The Music from* Fiorello!
(Verve 314 521 677-2)
'Til Tomorrow

Oscar Peterson Plays Porgy and Bess®   (Verve 314 519 807-2)
Summertime

The Oscar Peterson Trio at the Concertgebouw   (Verve 314 521 649-2)
The Lady Is a Tramp

All the Things You Are

from *VERY WARM FOR MAY*

Lyrics by Oscar Hammerstein II
Music by Jerome Kern

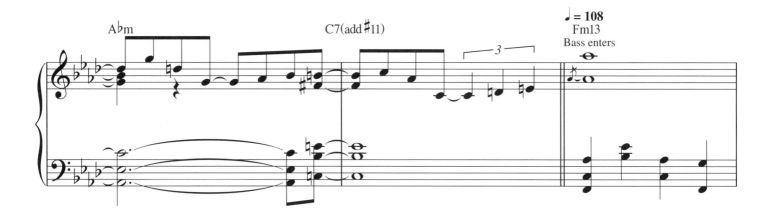

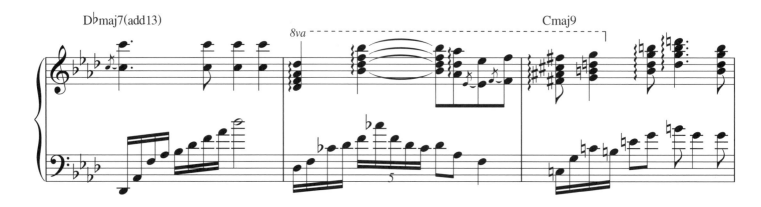

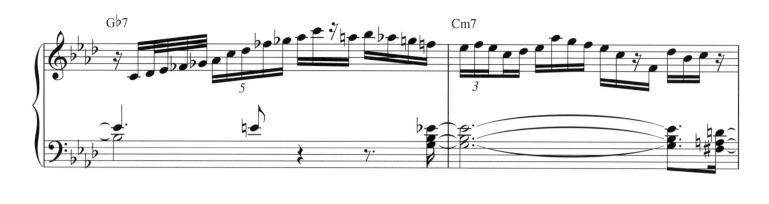

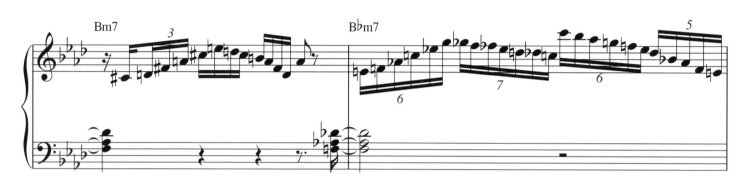

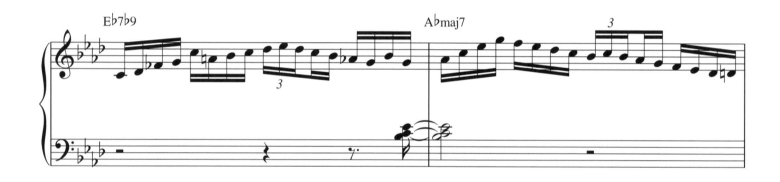

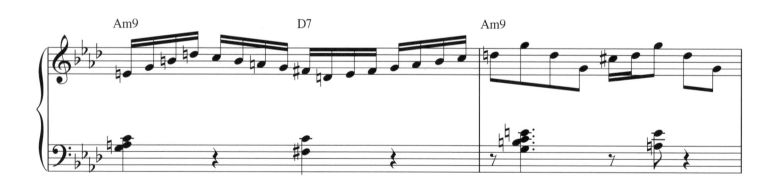

Baubles, Bangles and Beads

from *KISMET*

Words and Music by Robert Wright and George Forrest
(Music Based on Themes of A. Borodin)

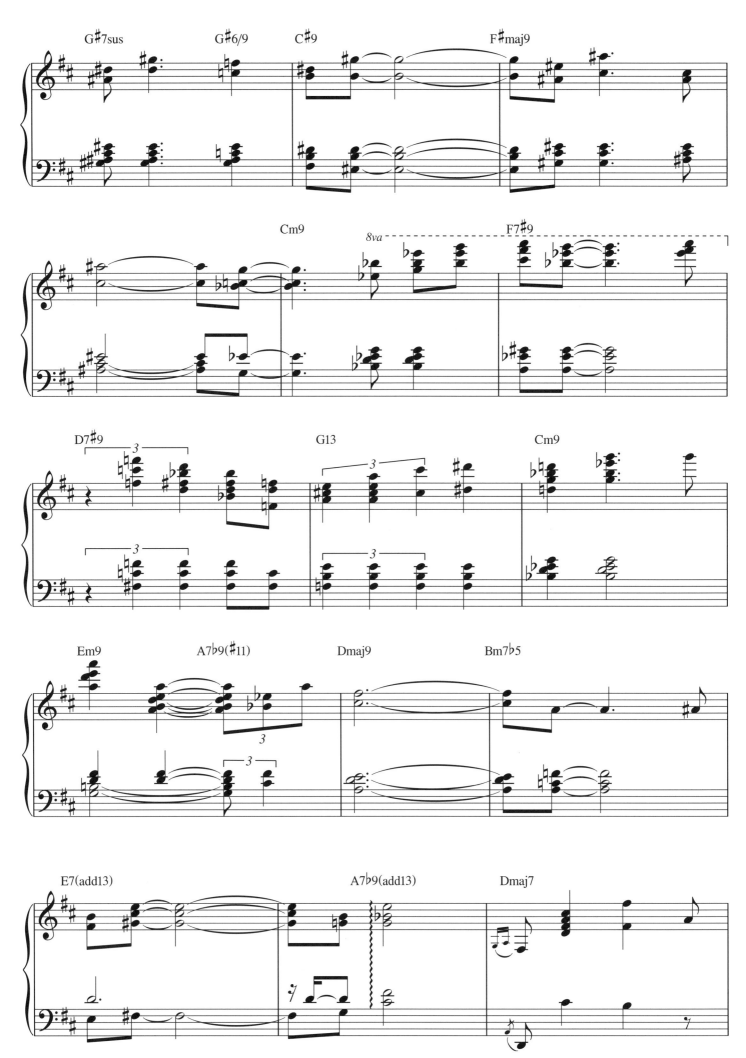

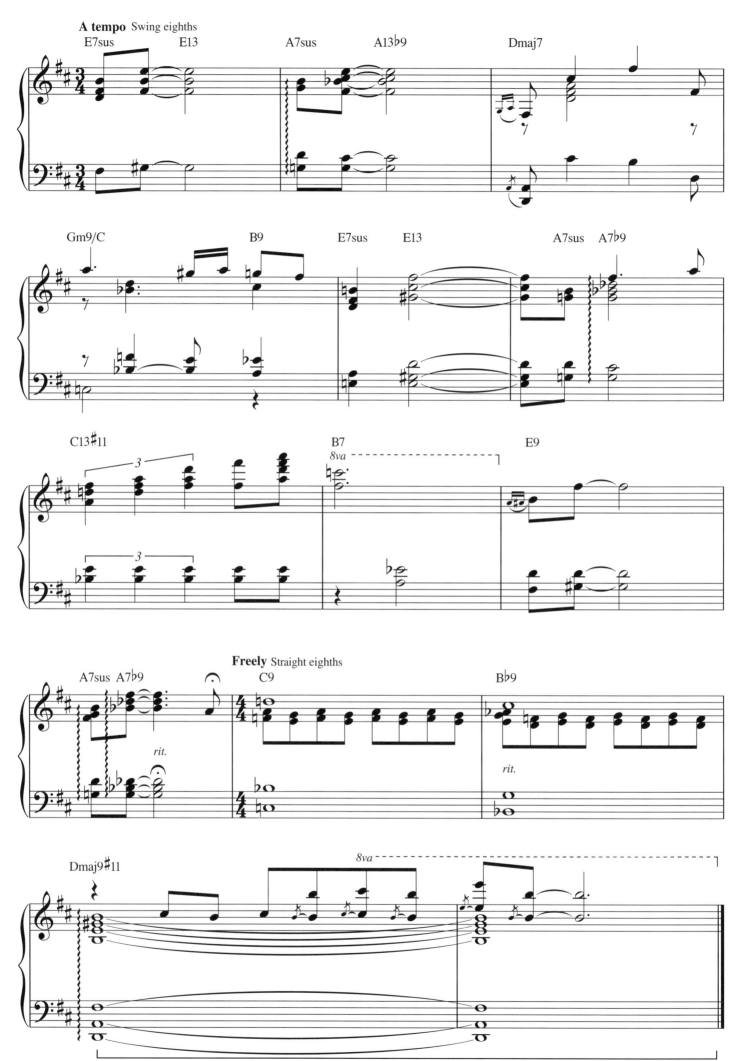

Body and Soul

Words by Edward Heyman, Robert Sour and Frank Eyton
Music by John Green

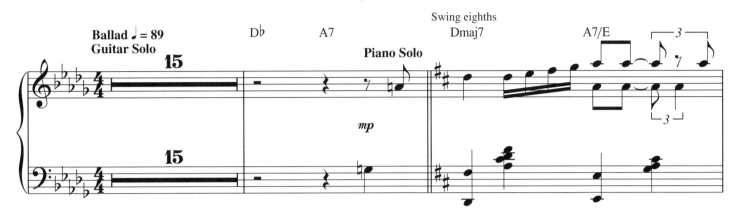

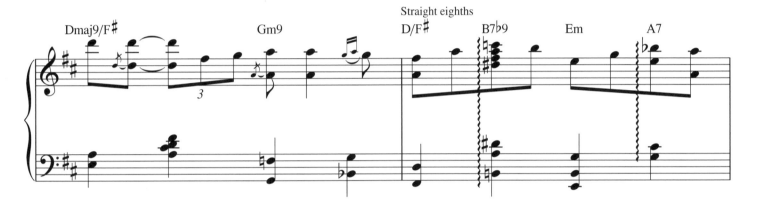

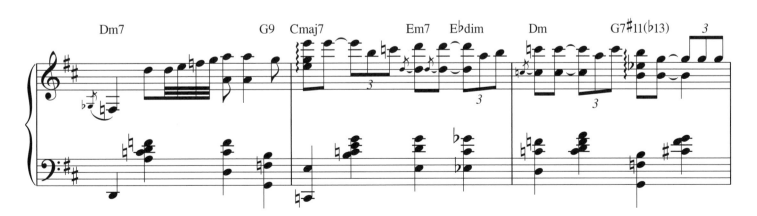

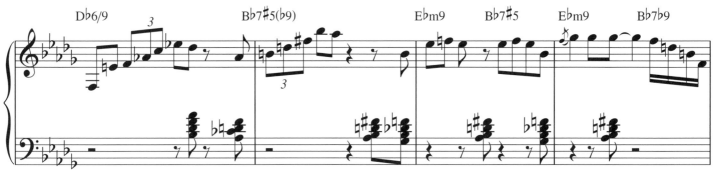

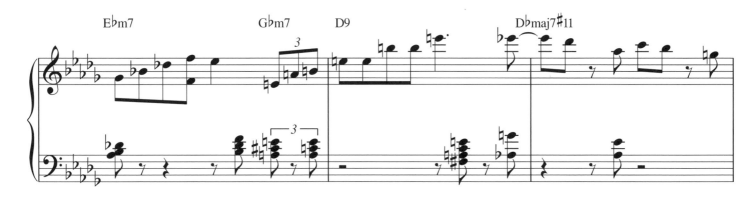

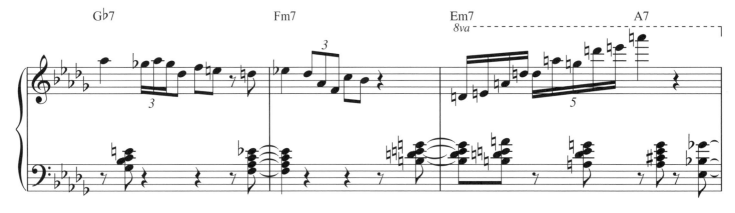

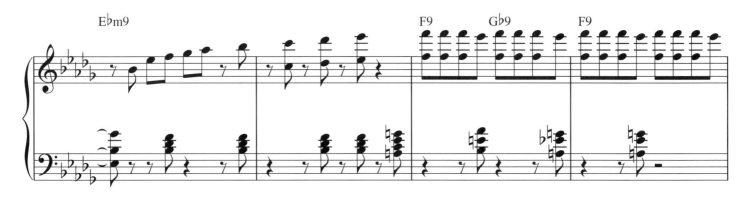

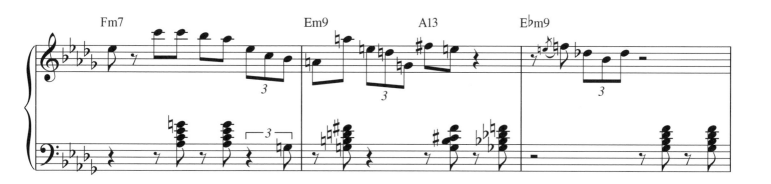

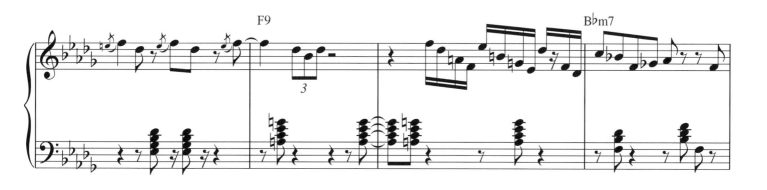

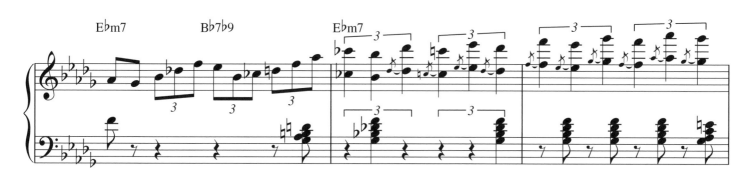

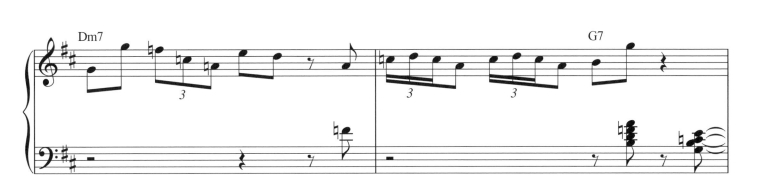

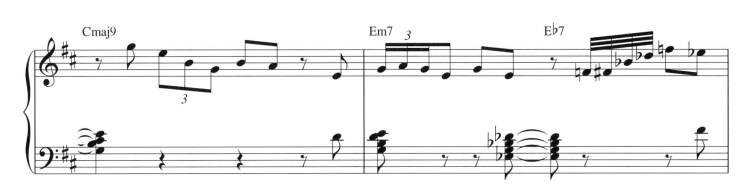

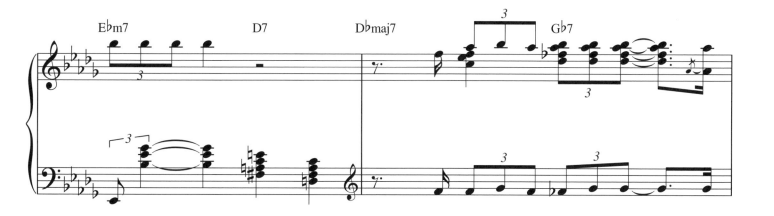

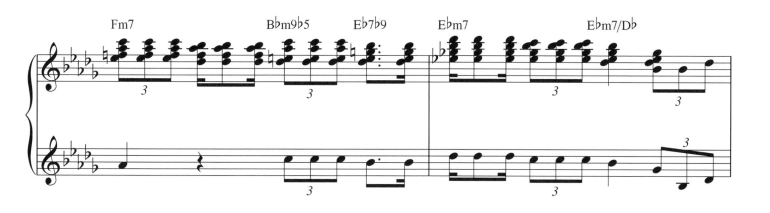

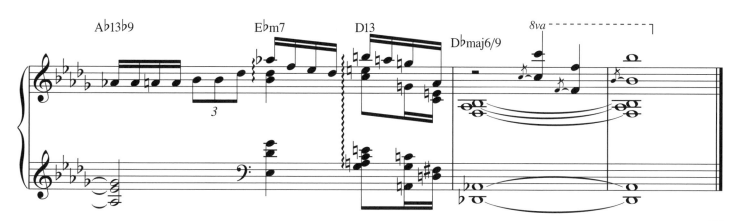

Come Rain or Come Shine
from *ST. LOUIS WOMAN*
Words by Johnny Mercer
Music by Harold Arlen

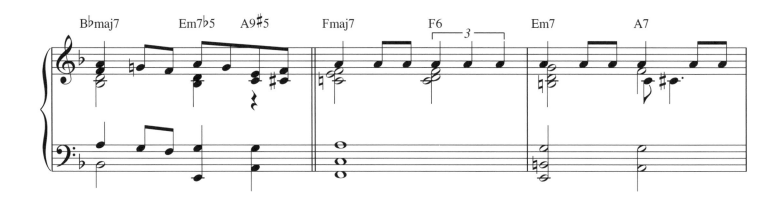

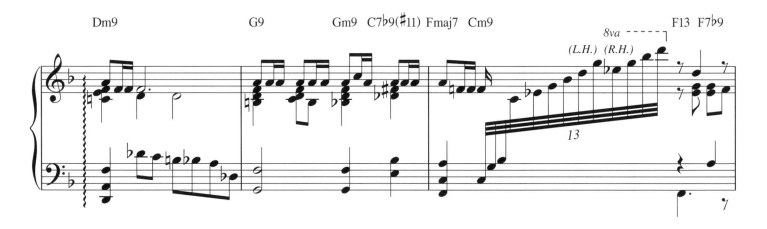

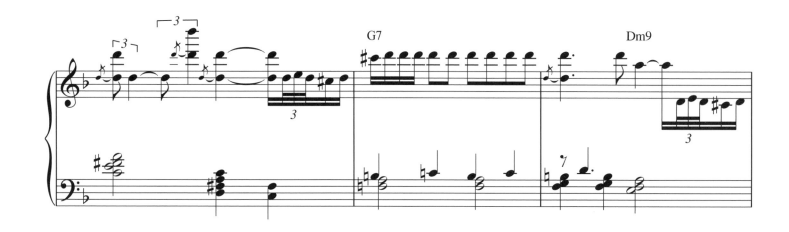

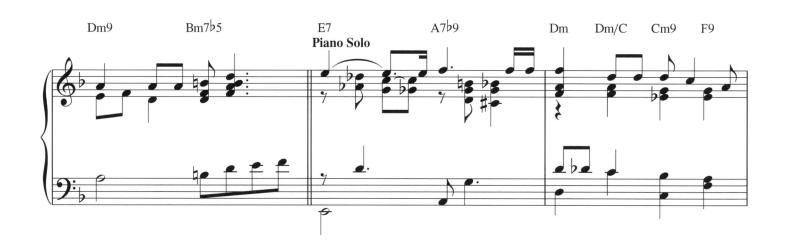

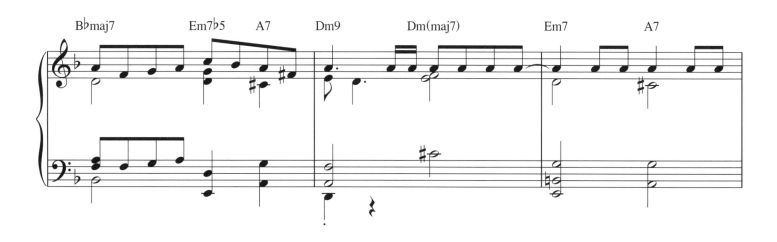

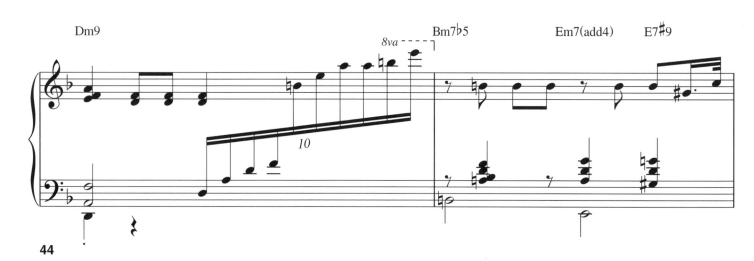

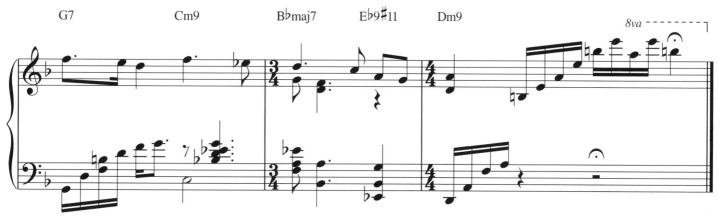

Easter Parade

featured in the Motion Picture Irving Berlin's *EASTER PARADE*
from *AS THOUSANDS CHEER*

Words and Music by Irving Berlin

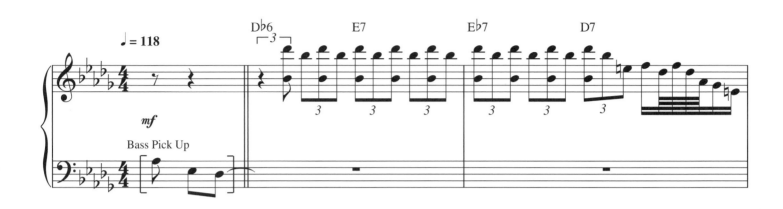

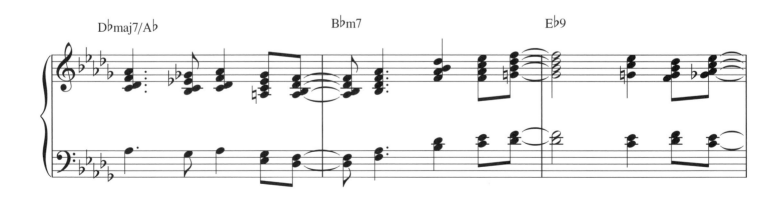

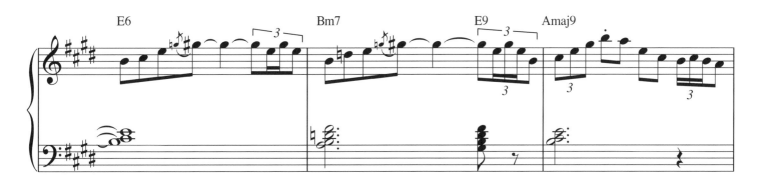

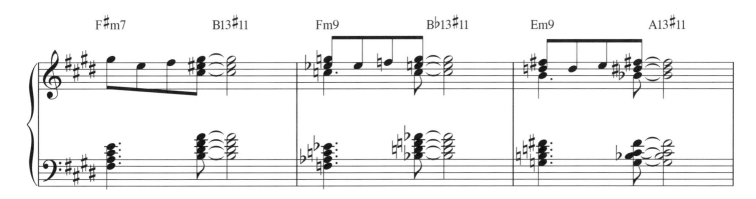

If I Were a Bell

from *GUYS AND DOLLS*

By Frank Loesser

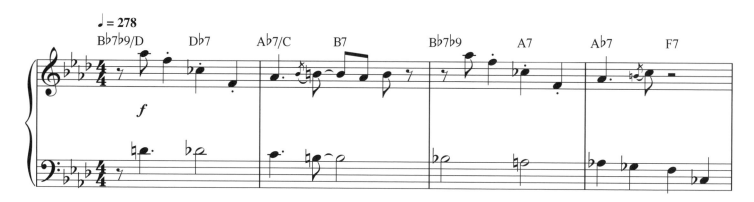

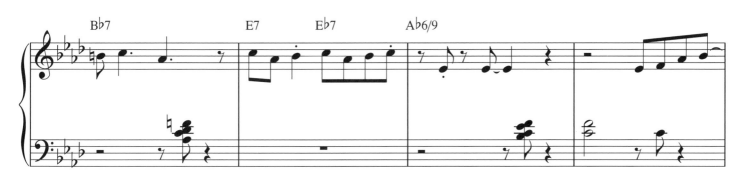

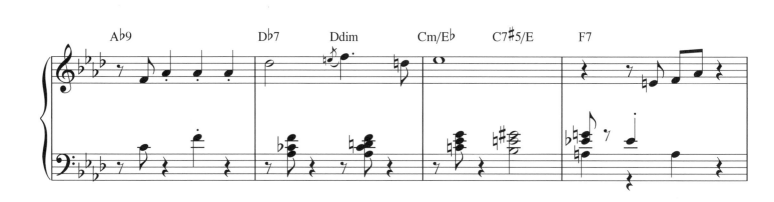

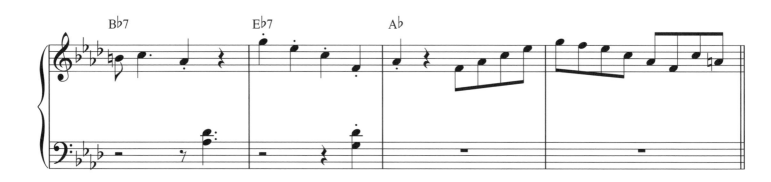

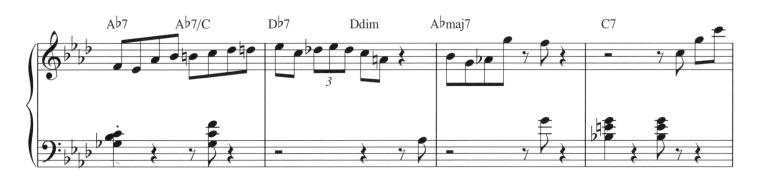

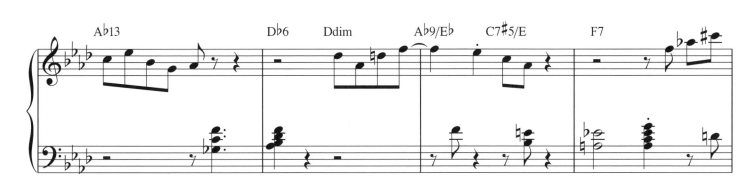

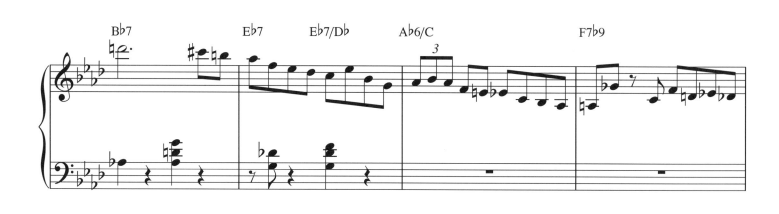

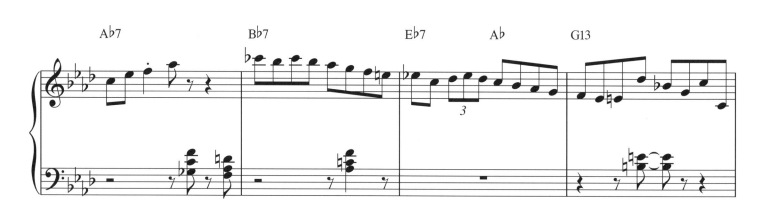

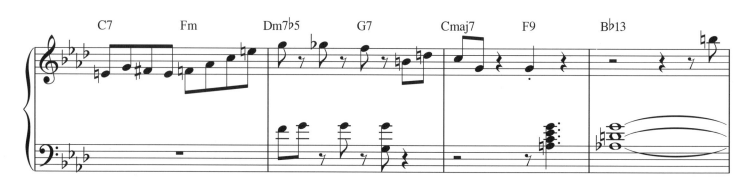

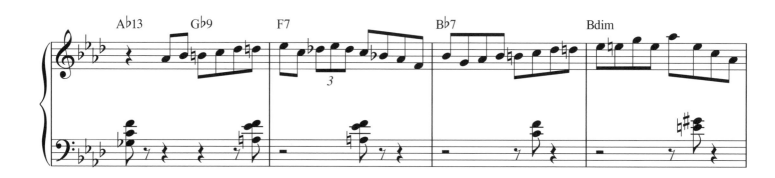

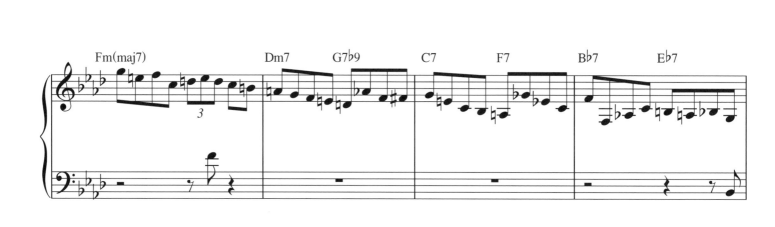

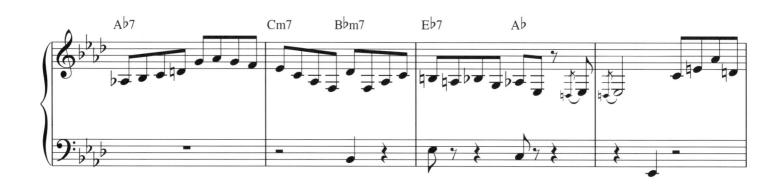

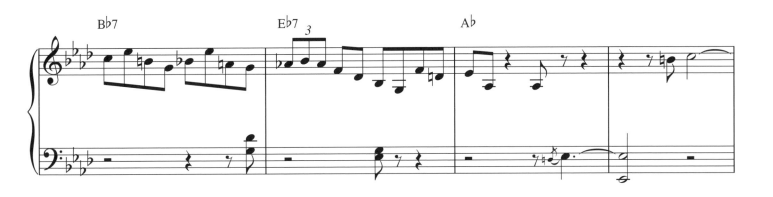

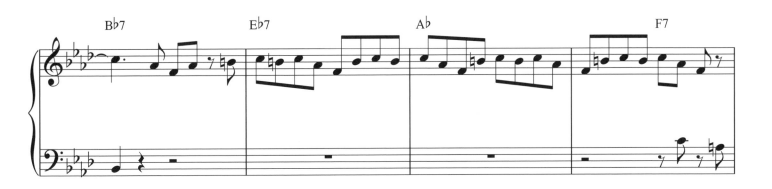

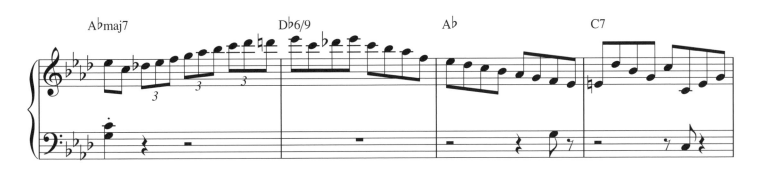

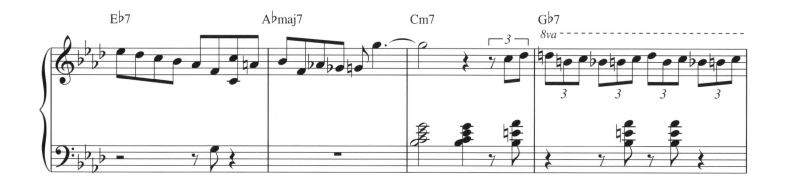

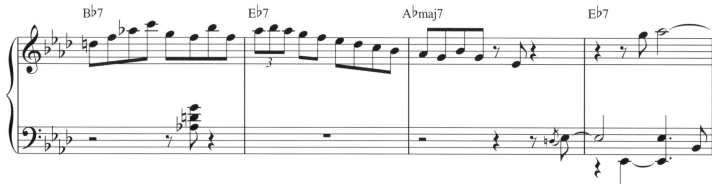

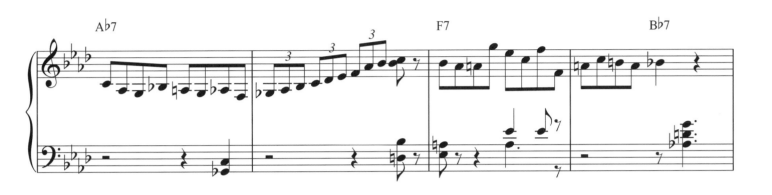

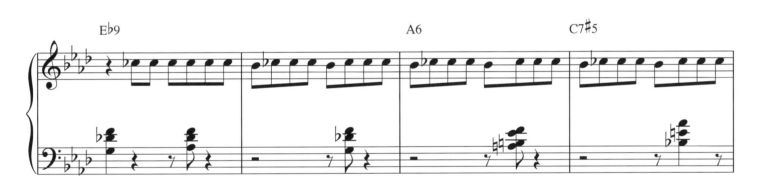

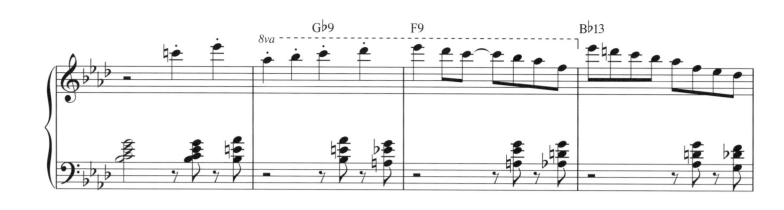

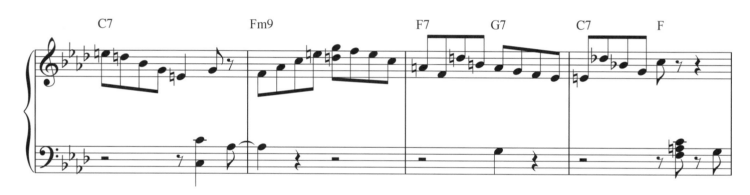

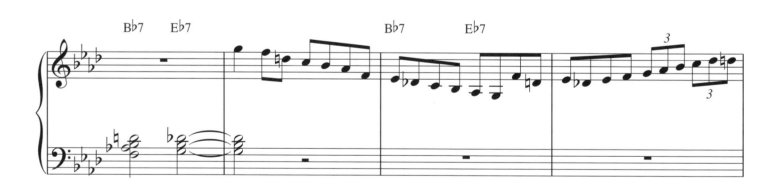

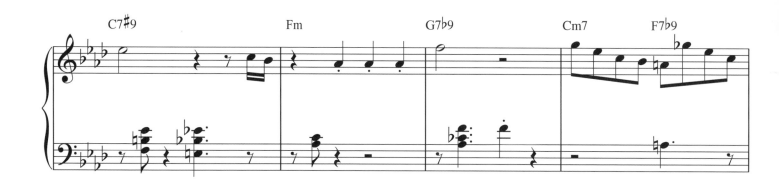

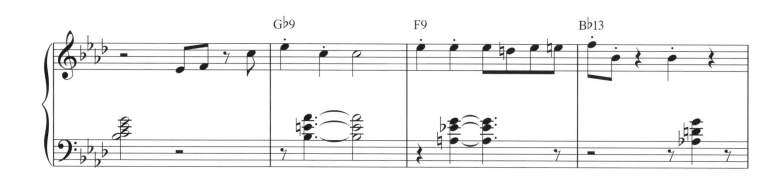

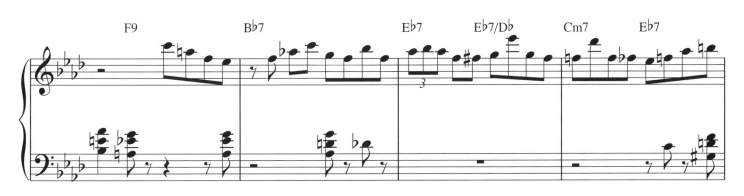

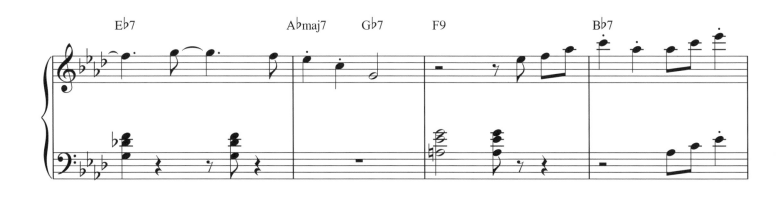

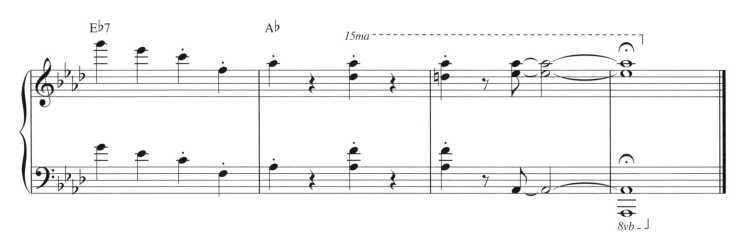

Just in Time

from *BELLS ARE RINGING*

Words by Betty Comden and Adolph Green
Music by Jule Styne

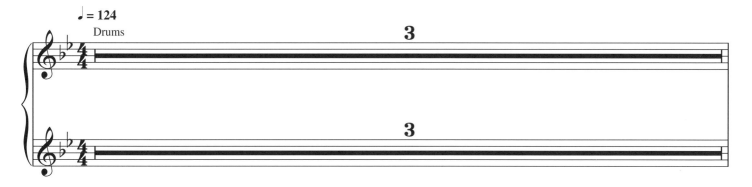

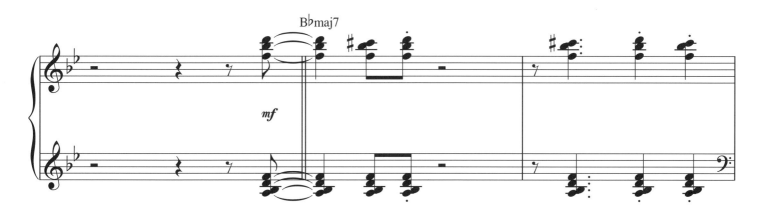

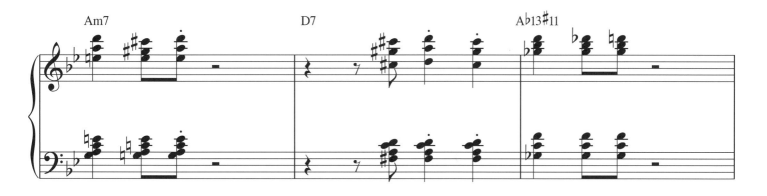

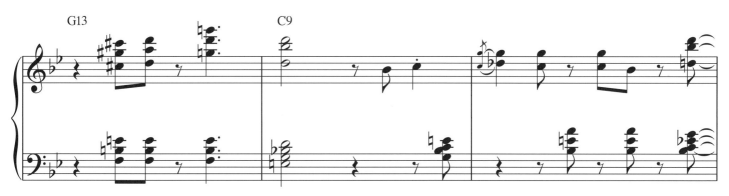

The Lady Is a Tramp

from *BABES IN ARMS*
from *WORDS AND MUSIC*
Words by Lorenz Hart
Music by Richard Rodgers

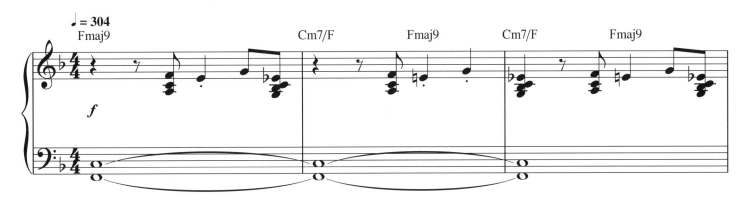

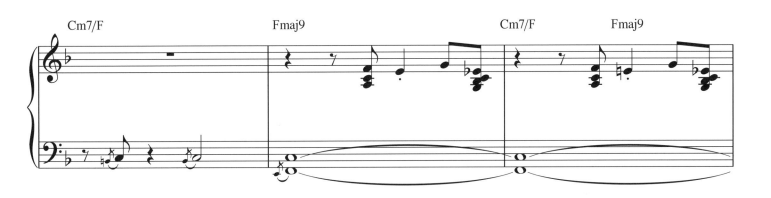

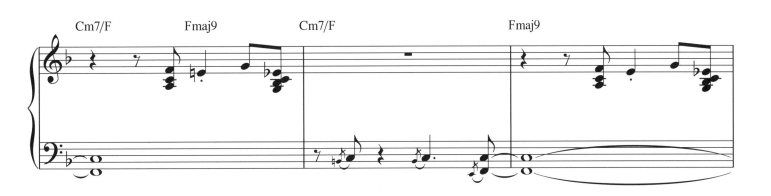

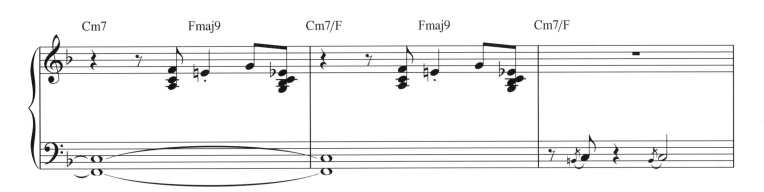

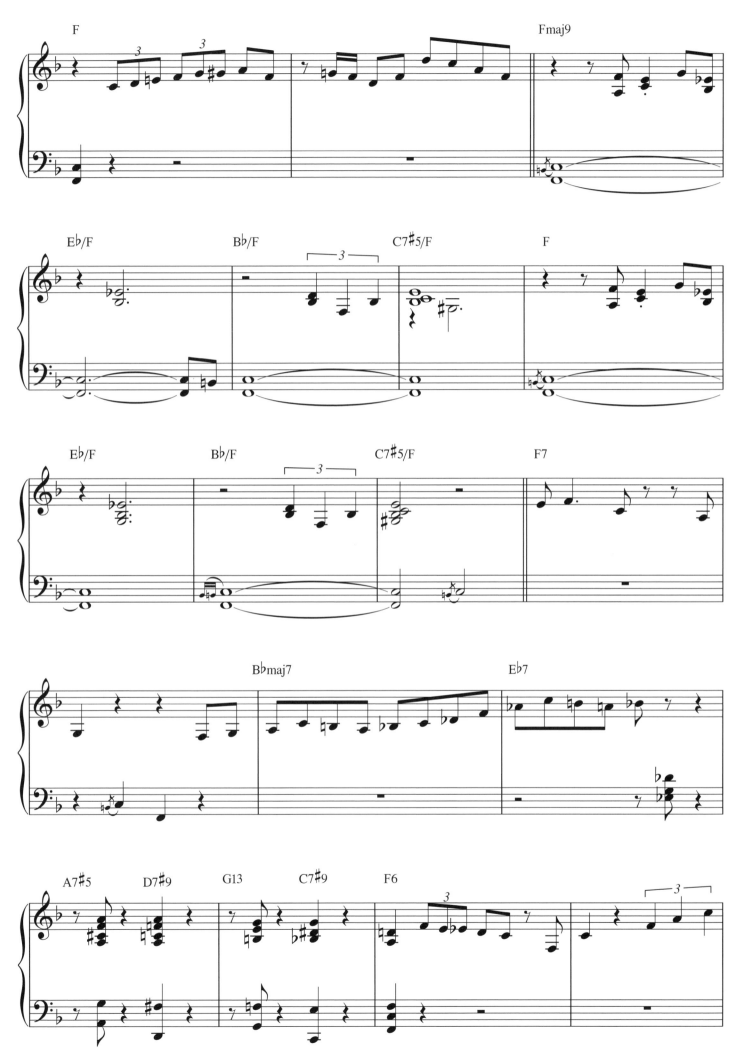

81

On a Clear Day
(You Can See Forever)
from *ON A CLEAR DAY YOU CAN SEE FOREVER*

Words by Alan Jay Lerner
Music by Burton Lane

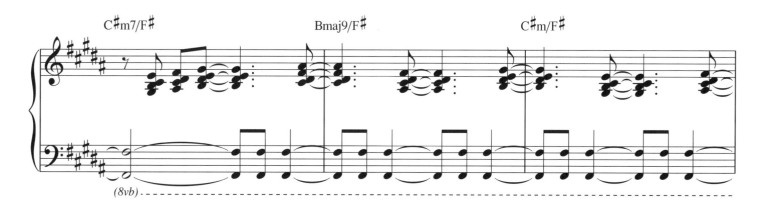

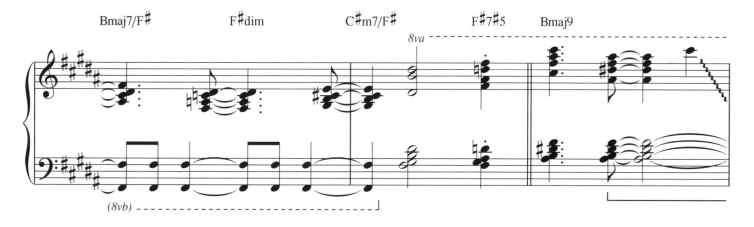

People

from *FUNNY GIRL*

Words by Bob Merrill
Music by Jule Styne

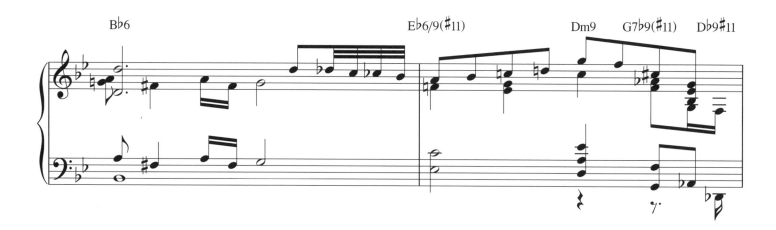

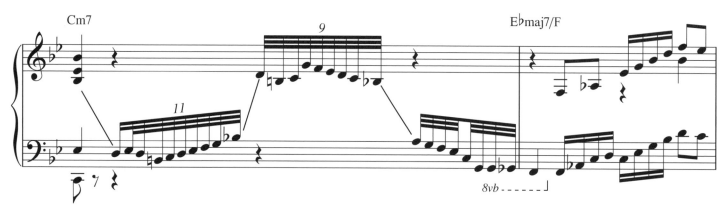

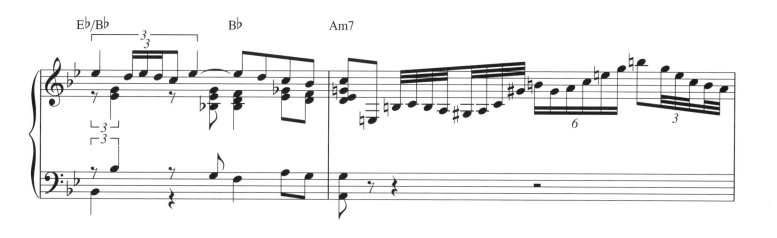

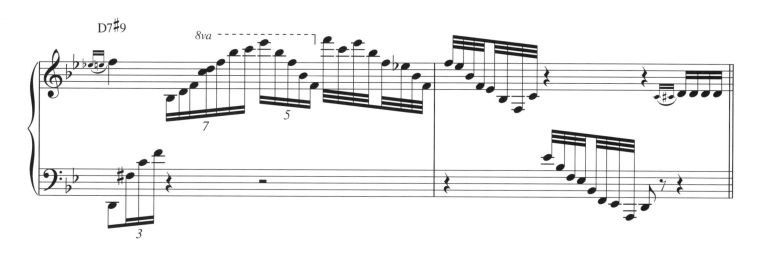

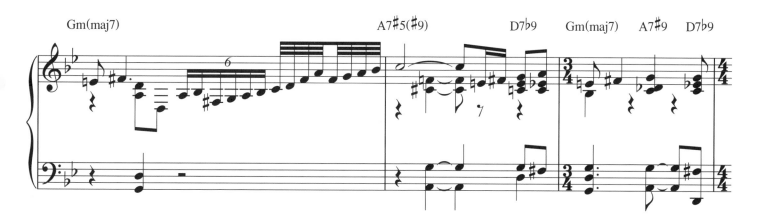

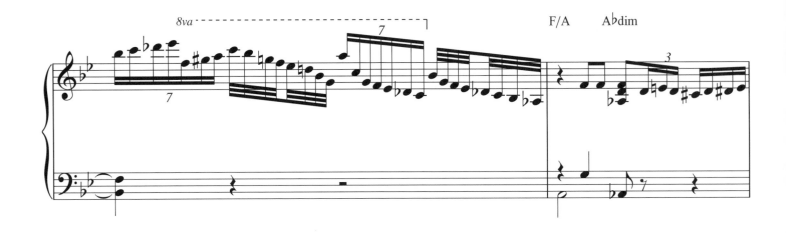

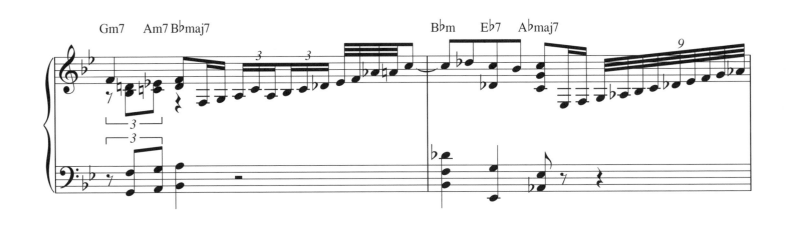

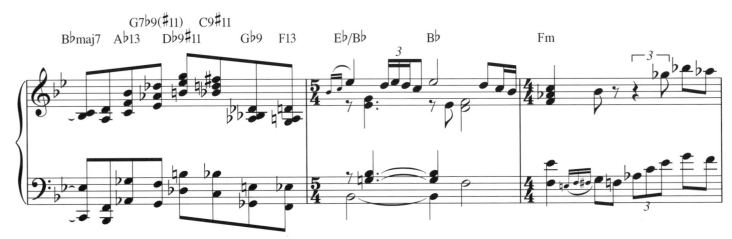

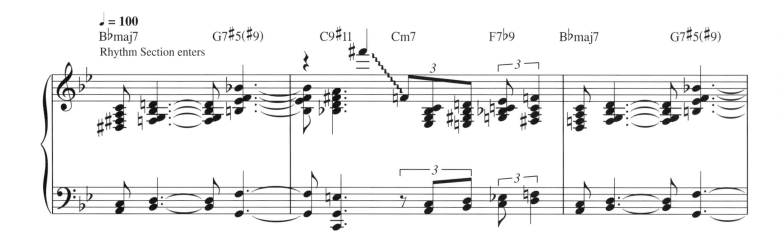

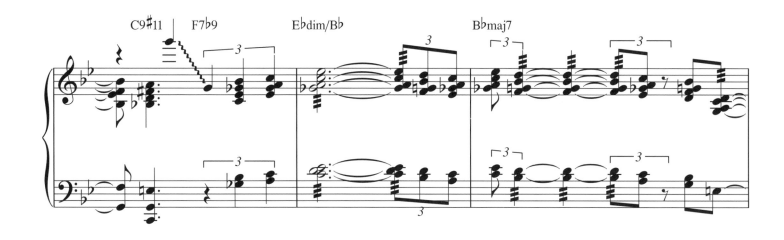

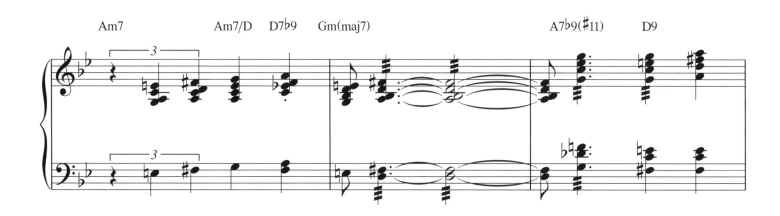

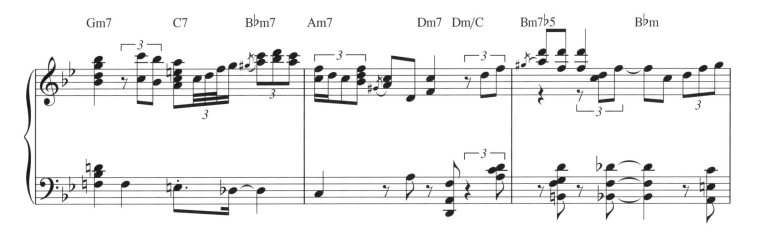

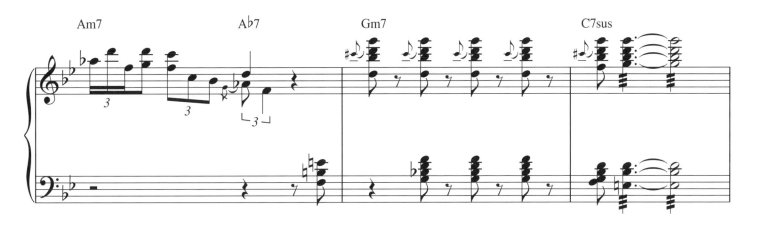

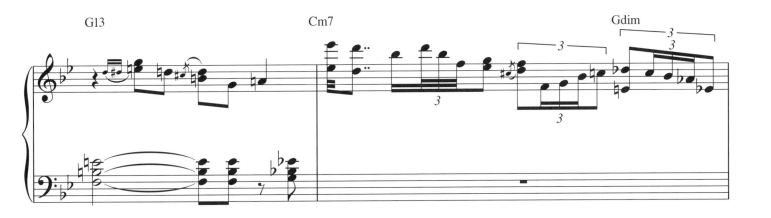

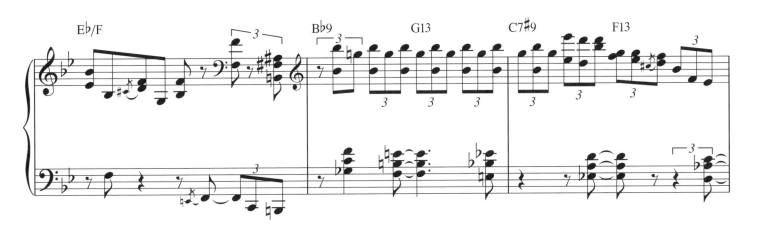

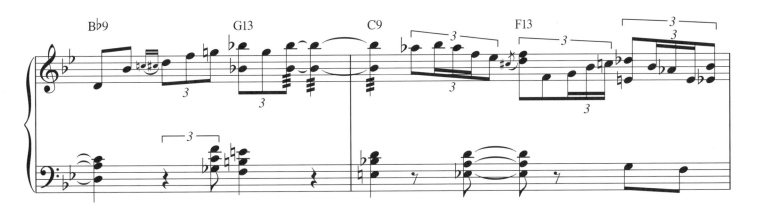

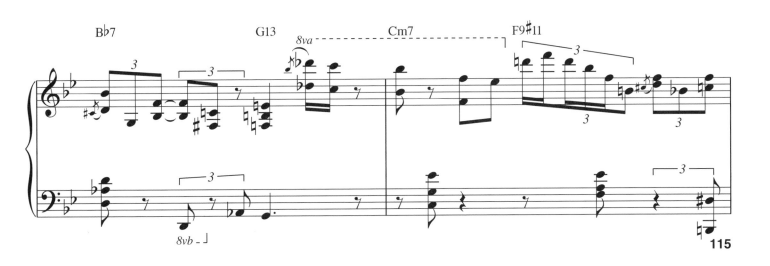

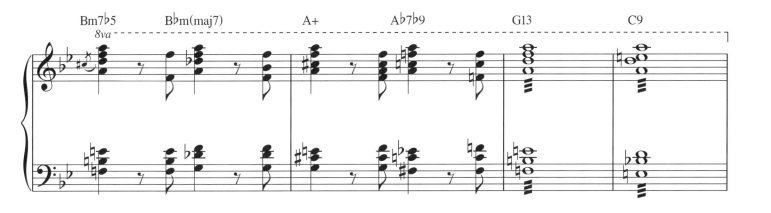

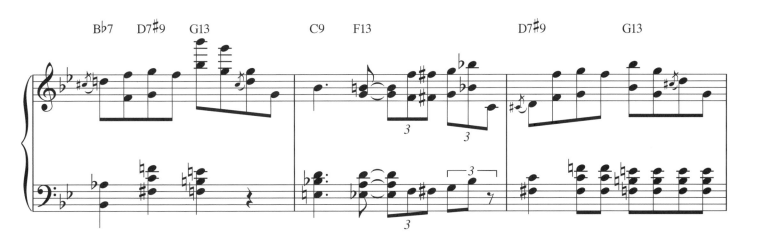

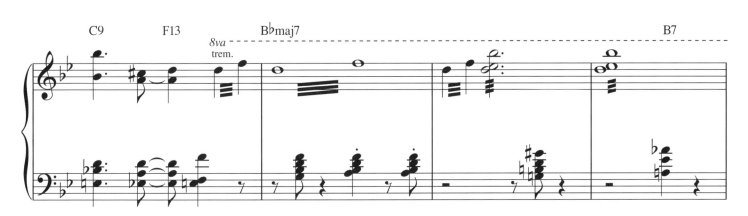

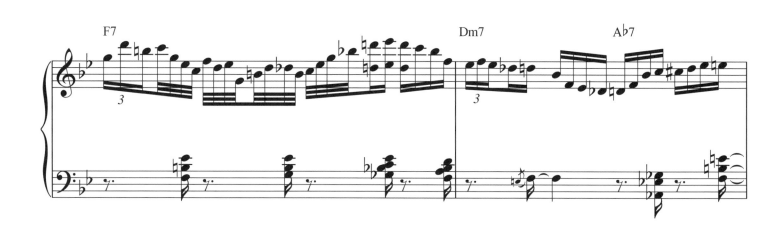

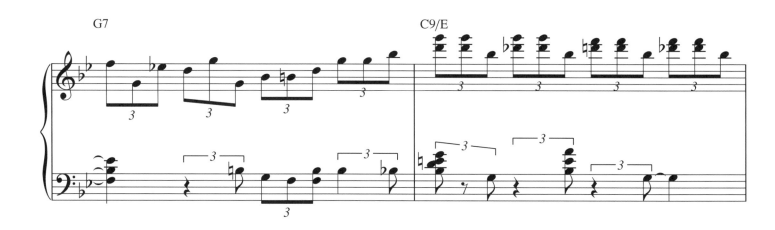

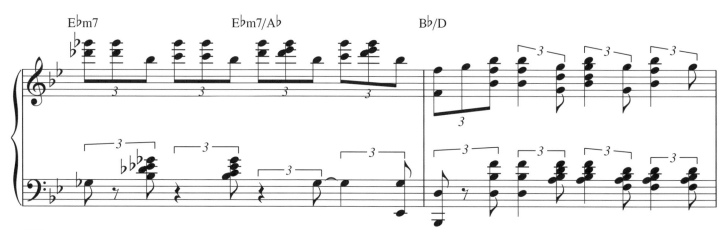

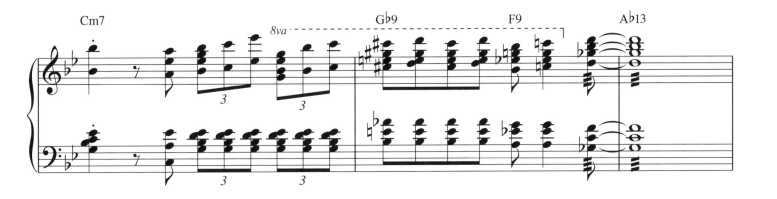

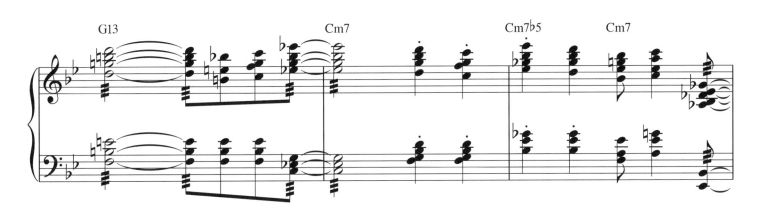

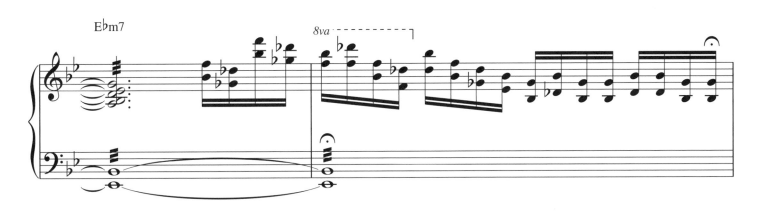

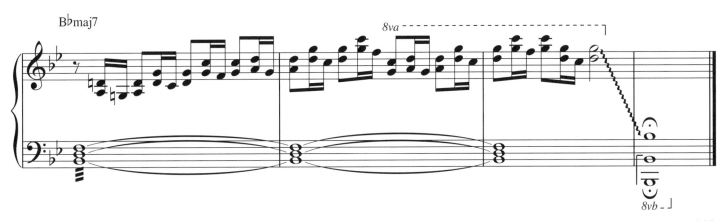

Strike Up the Band

from *STRIKE UP THE BAND*

Music and Lyrics by George Gershwin and Ira Gershwin

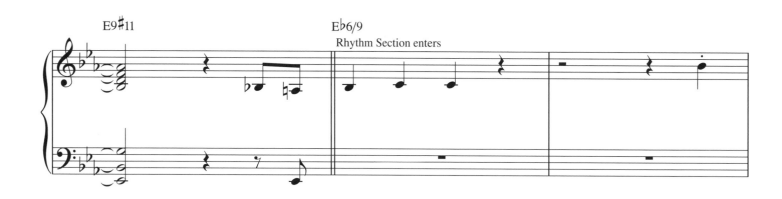

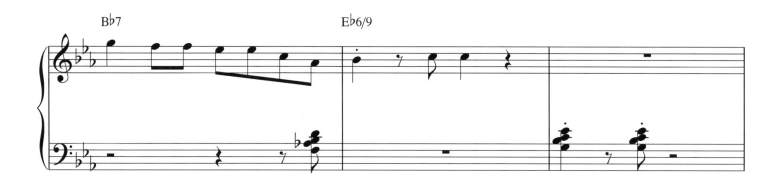

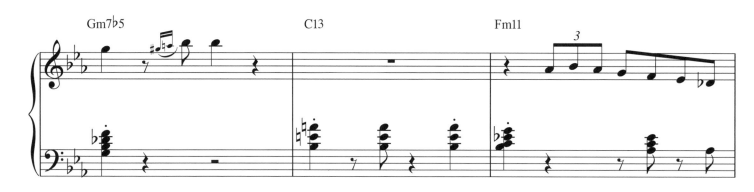

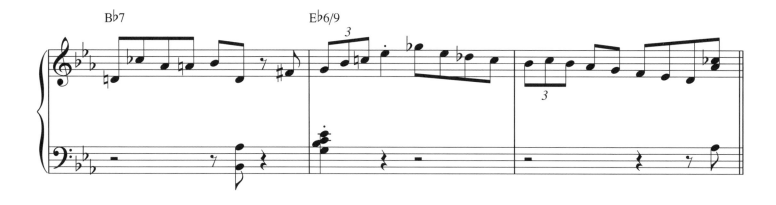

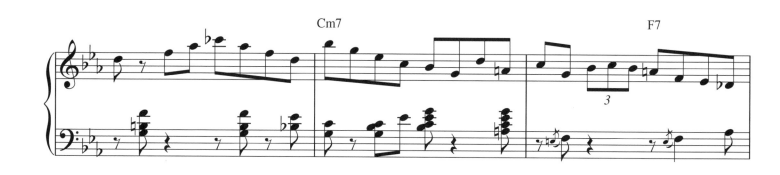

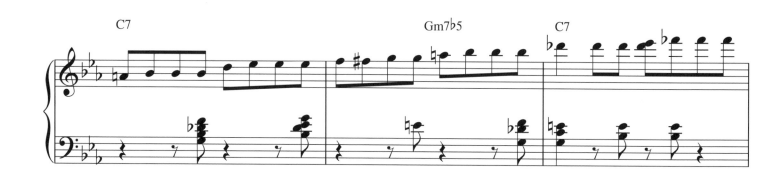

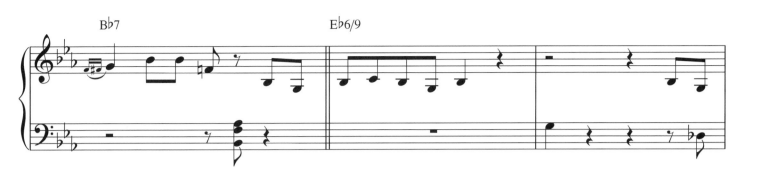

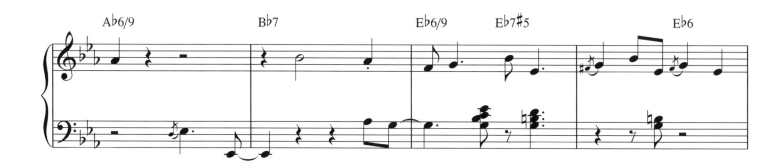

Summertime

from *PORGY AND BESS*®

Words and Music by George Gershwin, Du Bose and Dorothy Heyward and Ira Gershwin

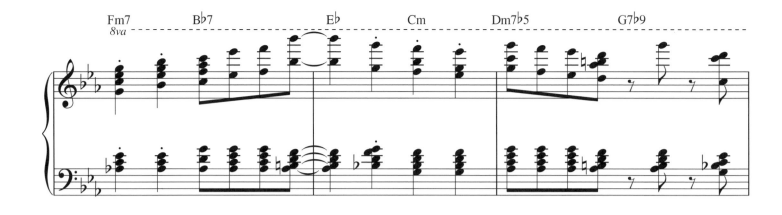

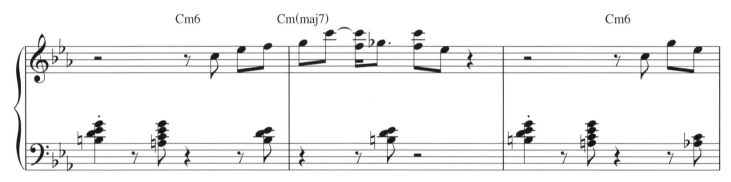

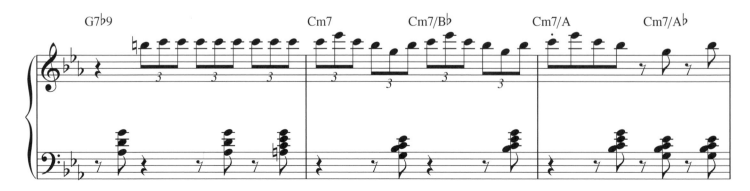

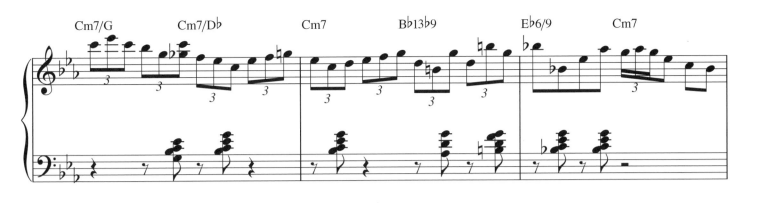

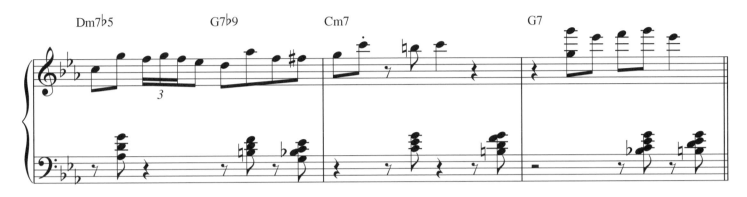

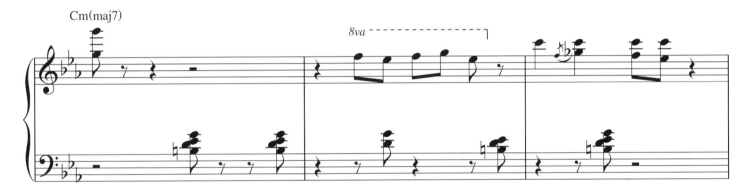

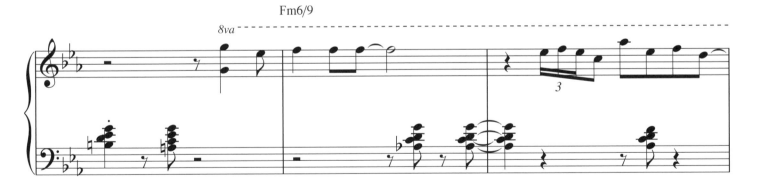

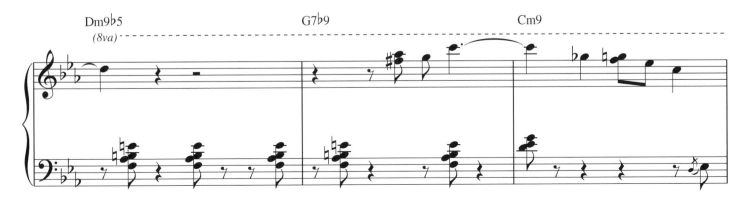

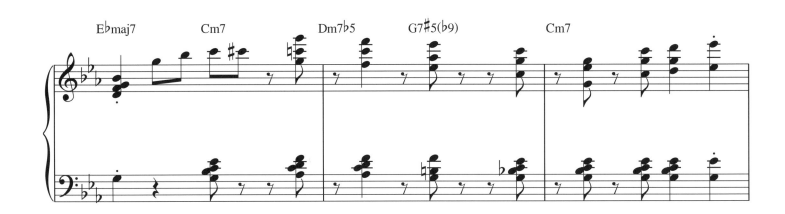

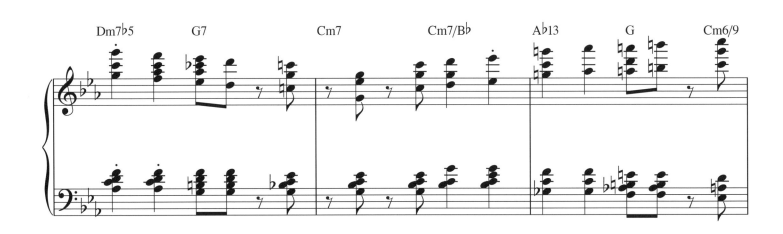

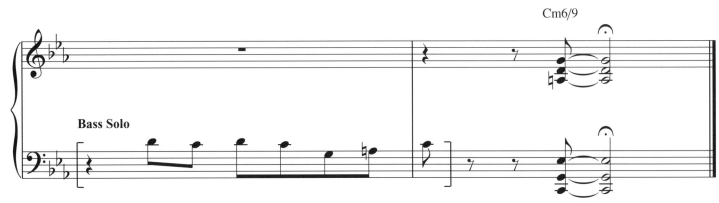

The Surrey with the Fringe on Top

from *OKLAHOMA!*

Lyrics by Oscar Hammerstein II
Music by Richard Rodgers

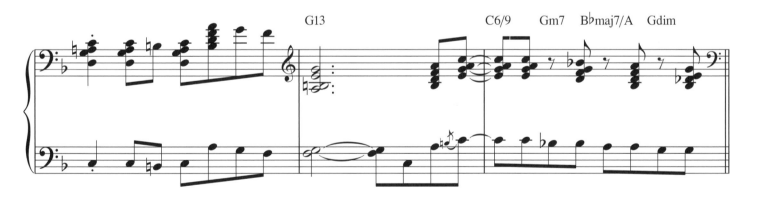

There's a Small Hotel

from *ON YOUR TOES*

Words by Lorenz Hart
Music by Richard Rodgers

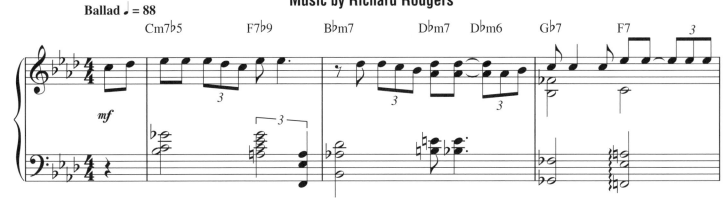

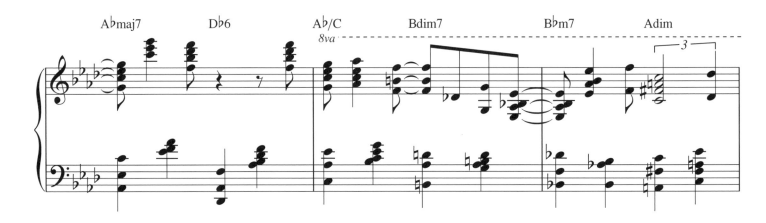

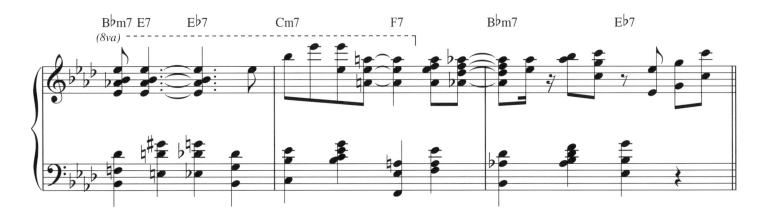

'Til Tomorrow

from the Musical *FIORELLO!*

Lyrics by Sheldon Harnick
Music by Jerry Bock

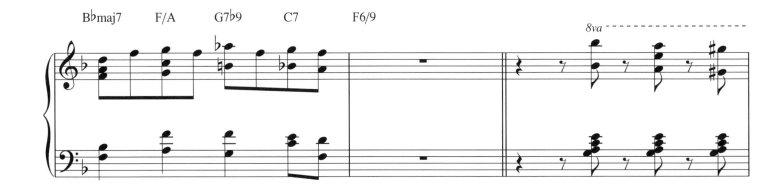

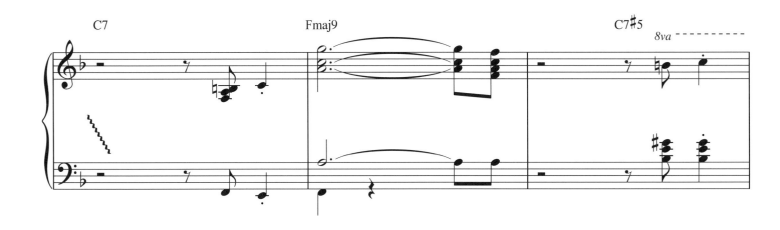

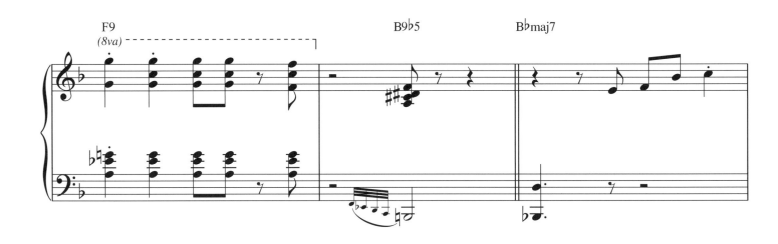

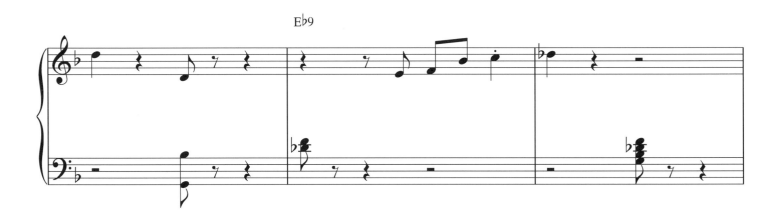

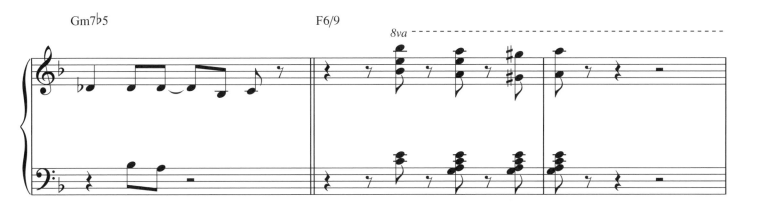

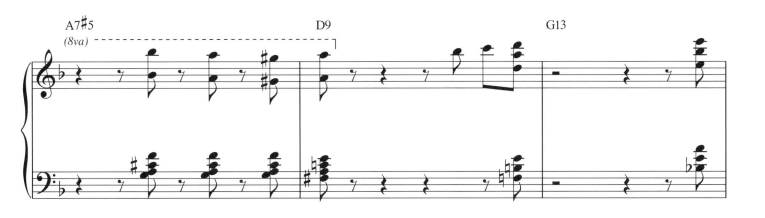

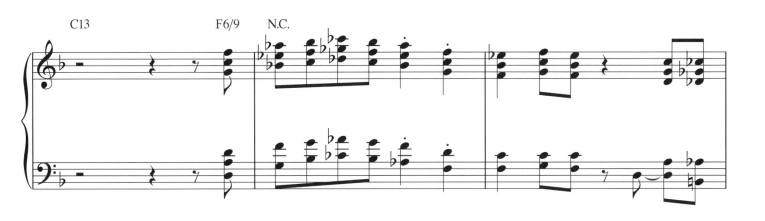

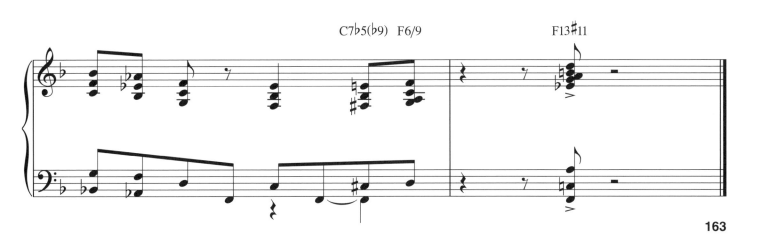

Who Can I Turn To

(When Nobody Needs Me)

from *THE ROAR OF THE GREASEPAINT—THE SMELL OF THE CROWD*

Words and Music by Leslie Bricusse and Anthony Newley

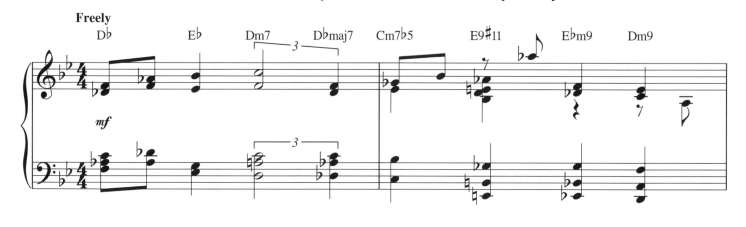

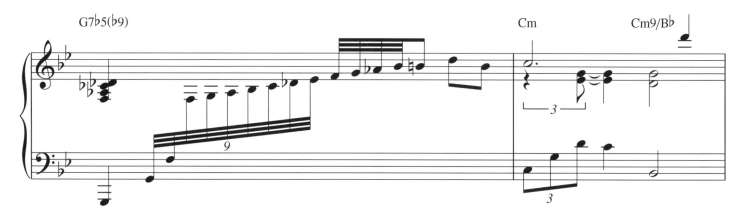

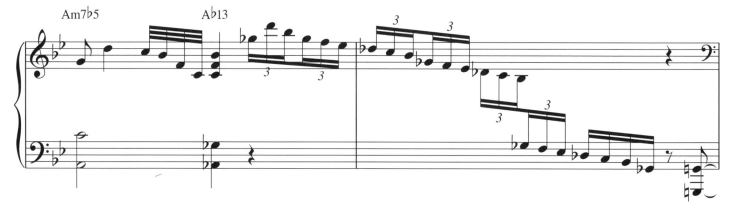

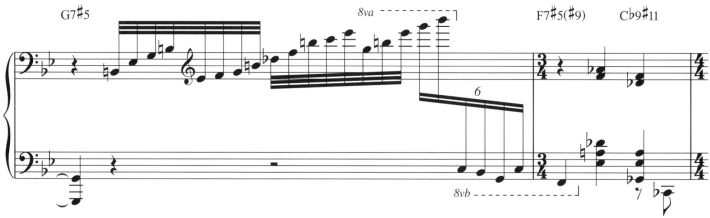

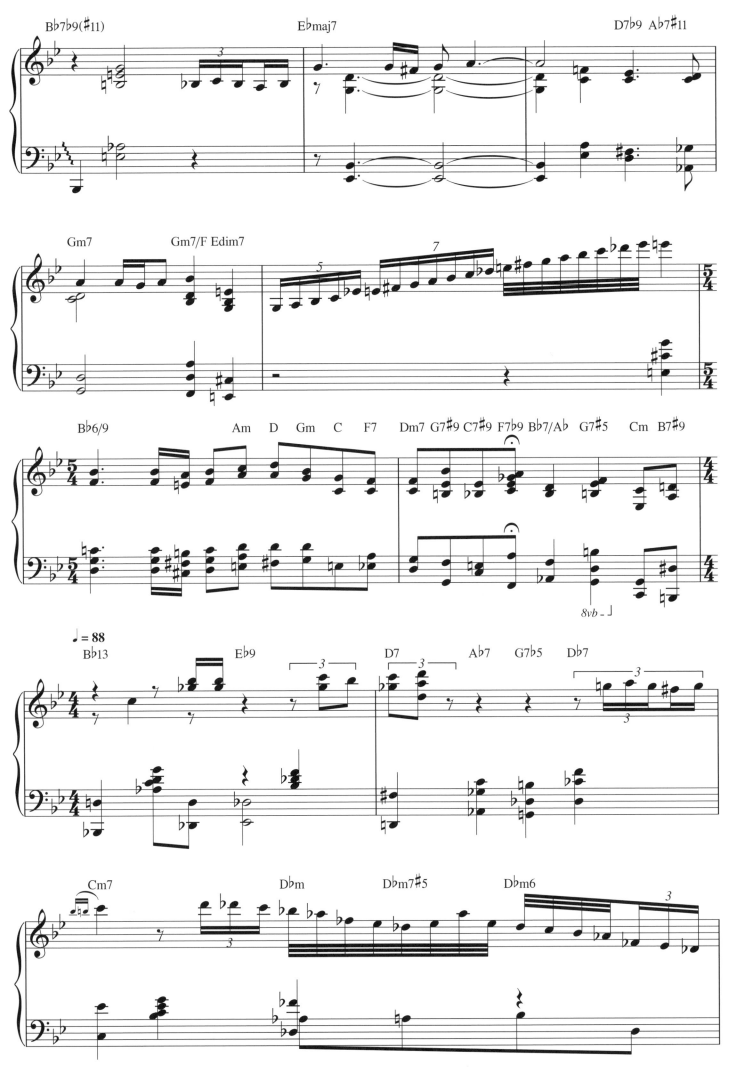

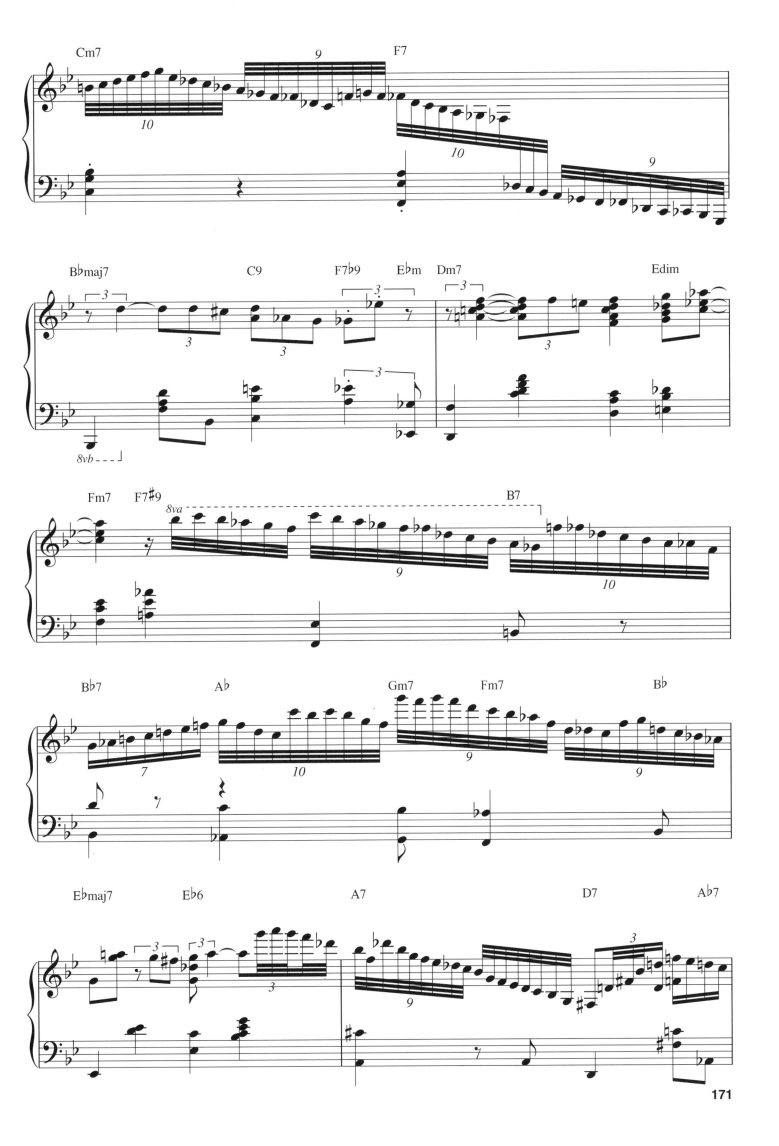

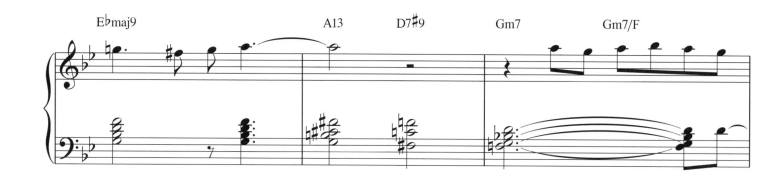

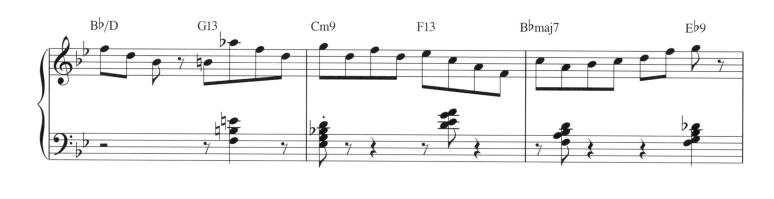

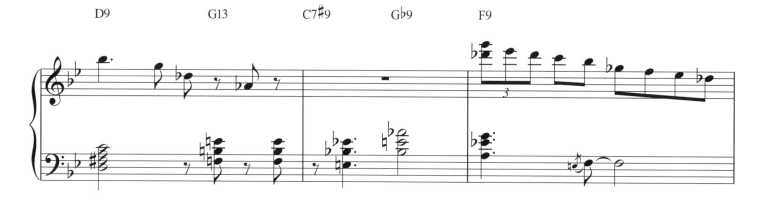

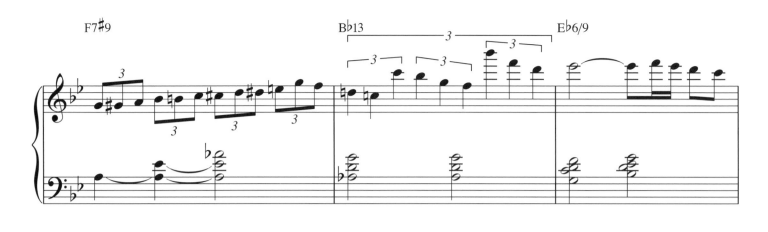

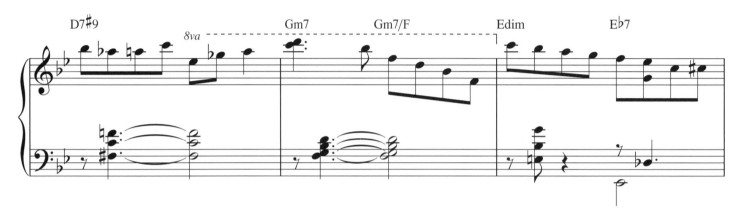

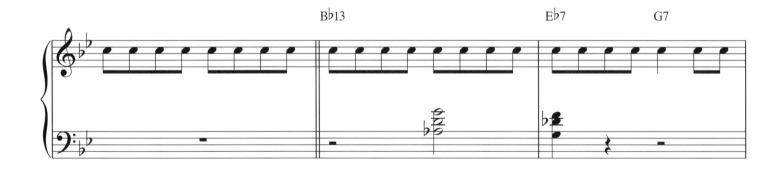

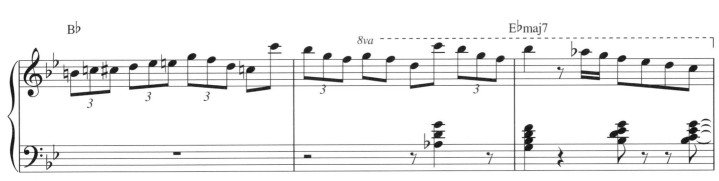

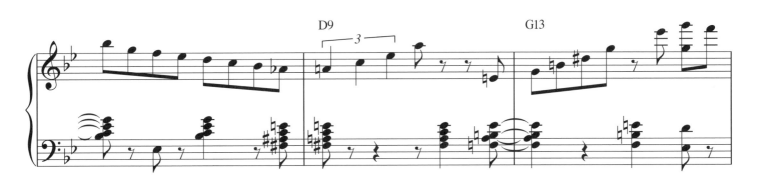

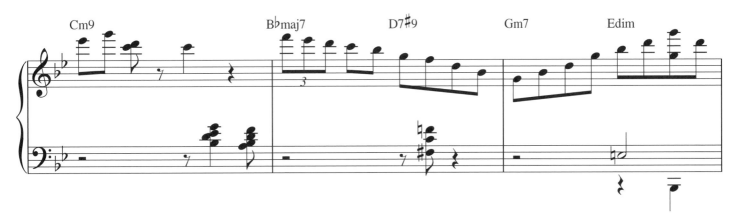

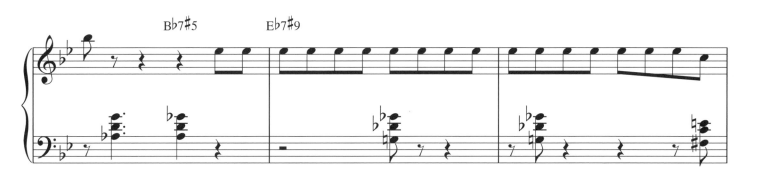

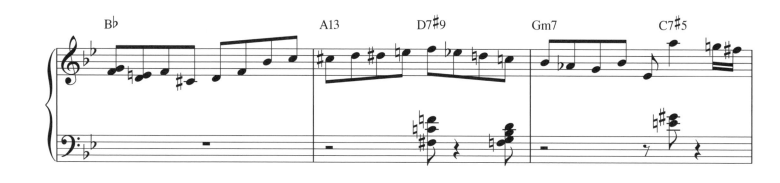

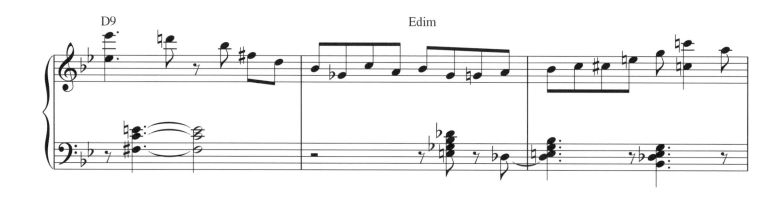

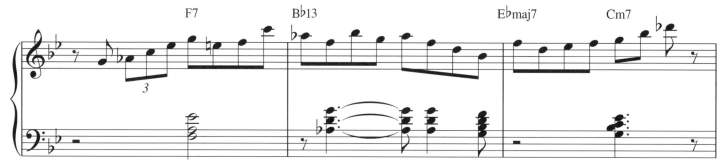

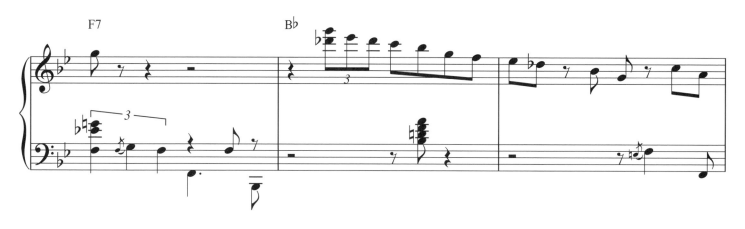

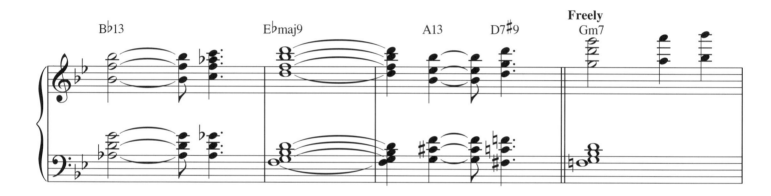

Wouldn't It Be Loverly

from *MY FAIR LADY*

Words by Alan Jay Lerner
Music by Frederick Loewe

Medium Swing ♩ = 108

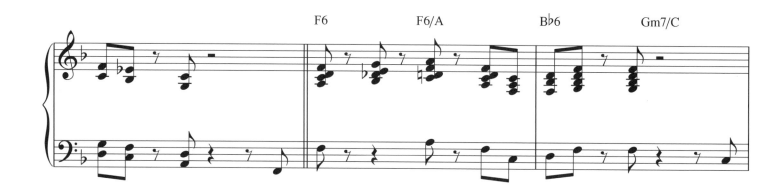

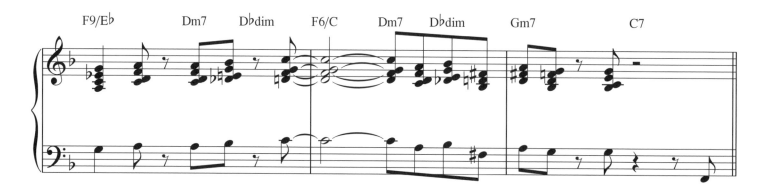

ARTIST TRANSCRIPTIONS®

Artist Transcriptions are authentic, note-for-note transcriptions of today's hottest artists in jazz, pop and rock. These outstanding, accurate arrangements are in an easy-to-read format which includes all essential lines. Artist Transcriptions can be used to perform, sequence or for reference.

CLARINET

00672423	Buddy De Franco Collection	$19.95

FLUTE

00672379	Eric Dolphy Collection	$19.95
00672372	James Moody Collection – Sax and Flute	$19.95
00660108	James Newton – Improvising Flute	$14.95
00672455	Lew Tabackin Collection	$19.95

GUITAR & BASS

00660113	The Guitar Style of George Benson	$14.95
00672331	Ron Carter – Acoustic Bass	$16.95
00660115	Al Di Meola – Friday Night in San Francisco	$14.95
00604043	Al Di Meola – Music, Words, Pictures	$14.95
00673245	Jazz Style of Tal Farlow	$19.95
00672359	Bela Fleck and the Flecktones	$18.95
00699389	Jim Hall – Jazz Guitar Environments	$19.95
00699306	Jim Hall – Exploring Jazz Guitar	$19.95
00672335	Best of Scott Henderson	$24.95
00672356	Jazz Guitar Standards	$19.95
00675536	Wes Montgomery – Guitar Transcriptions	$17.95
00672353	Joe Pass Collection	$18.95
00673216	John Patitucci	$16.95
00672374	Johnny Smith Guitar Solos	$16.95
00672320	Mark Whitfield	$19.95
00672337	Gary Willis Collection	$19.95

PIANO & KEYBOARD

00672338	Monty Alexander Collection	$19.95
00672487	Monty Alexander Plays Standards	$19.95
00672318	Kenny Barron Collection	$22.95
00672520	Count Basie Collection	$19.95
00672364	Warren Bernhardt Collection	$19.95
00672439	Cyrus Chestnut Collection	$19.95
00673242	Billy Childs Collection	$19.95
00672300	Chick Corea – Paint the World	$12.95
00672537	Bill Evans at Town Hall	$16.95
00672425	Bill Evans – Piano Interpretations	$19.95
00672365	Bill Evans – Piano Standards	$19.95
00672510	Bill Evans Trio – Vol. 1: 1959-1961	$24.95
00672511	Bill Evans Trio – Vol. 2: 1962-1965	$24.95
00672512	Bill Evans Trio – Vol. 3: 1968-1974	$24.95
00672513	Bill Evans Trio – Vol. 4: 1979-1980	$24.95
00672329	Benny Green Collection	$19.95
00672486	Vince Guaraldi Collection	$19.95
00672419	Herbie Hancock Collection	$19.95
00672446	Gene Harris Collection	$19.95
00672438	Hampton Hawes	$19.95
00672322	Ahmad Jamal Collection	$22.95
00672476	Brad Mehldau Collection	$19.95

00672390	Thelonious Monk Plays Jazz Standards – Volume 1	$19.95
00672391	Thelonious Monk Plays Jazz Standards – Volume 2	$19.95
00672433	Jelly Roll Morton – The Piano Rolls	$12.95
00672542	Oscar Peterson – Jazz Piano Solos	$14.95
00672544	Oscar Peterson – Originals	$9.95
00672532	Oscar Peterson – Plays Broadway	$19.95
00672531	Oscar Peterson – Plays Duke Ellington	$19.95
00672533	Oscar Peterson – Trios	$24.95
00672543	Oscar Peterson Trio – Canadiana Suite	$7.95
00672534	Very Best of Oscar Peterson	$22.95
00672371	Bud Powell Classics	$19.95
00672376	Bud Powell Collection	$19.95
00672437	André Previn Collection	$19.95
00672507	Gonzalo Rubalcaba Collection	$19.95
00672303	Horace Silver Collection	$19.95
00672316	Art Tatum Collection	$22.95
00672355	Art Tatum Solo Book	$19.95
00672357	Billy Taylor Collection	$24.95
00673215	McCoy Tyner	$16.95
00672321	Cedar Walton Collection	$19.95
00672519	Kenny Werner Collection	$19.95
00672434	Teddy Wilson Collection	$19.95

SAXOPHONE

00673244	Julian "Cannonball" Adderley Collection	$19.95
00673237	Michael Brecker	$19.95
00672429	Michael Brecker Collection	$19.95
00672351	Brecker Brothers... And All Their Jazz	$19.95
00672447	Best of the Brecker Brothers	$19.95
00672315	Benny Carter Plays Standards	$22.95
00672314	Benny Carter Collection	$22.95
00672394	James Carter Collection	$19.95
00672349	John Coltrane Plays Giant Steps	$19.95
00672529	John Coltrane – Giant Steps	$14.95
00672494	John Coltrane – A Love Supreme	$14.95
00672493	John Coltrane Plays "Coltrane Changes"	$19.95
00672453	John Coltrane Plays Standards	$19.95
00673233	John Coltrane Solos	$22.95
00672328	Paul Desmond Collection	$19.95
00672454	Paul Desmond – Standard Time	$19.95
00672379	Eric Dolphy Collection	$19.95
00672530	Kenny Garrett Collection	$19.95
00699375	Stan Getz	$18.95
00672377	Stan Getz – Bossa Novas	$19.95
00672375	Stan Getz – Standards	$17.95
00673254	Great Tenor Sax Solos	$18.95
00672523	Coleman Hawkins Collection	$19.95
00673252	Joe Henderson – Selections from "Lush Life" & "So Near So Far"	$19.95
00672330	Best of Joe Henderson	$22.95

00673239	Best of Kenny G	$19.95
00673229	Kenny G – Breathless	$19.95
00672462	Kenny G – Classics in the Key of G	$19.95
00672485	Kenny G – Faith: A Holiday Album	$14.95
00672373	Kenny G – The Moment	$19.95
00672516	Kenny G – Paradise	$14.95
00672326	Joe Lovano Collection	$19.95
00672498	Jackie McLean Collection	$19.95
00672372	James Moody Collection – Sax and Flute	$19.95
00672416	Frank Morgan Collection	$19.95
00672539	Gerry Mulligan Collection	$19.95
00672352	Charlie Parker Collection	$19.95
00672444	Sonny Rollins Collection	$19.95
00675000	David Sanborn Collection	$16.95
00672528	Bud Shank Collection	$19.95
00672491	New Best of Wayne Shorter	$19.95
00672455	Lew Tabackin Collection	$19.95
00672334	Stanley Turrentine Collection	$19.95
00672524	Lester Young Collection	$19.95

TROMBONE

00672332	J.J. Johnson Collection	$19.95
00672489	Steve Turré Collection	$19.95

TRUMPET

00672480	Louis Armstrong Collection	$14.95
00672481	Louis Armstrong Plays Standards	$14.95
00672435	Chet Baker Collection	$19.95
00673234	Randy Brecker	$17.95
00672351	Brecker Brothers... And All Their Jazz	$19.95
00672447	Best of the Brecker Brothers	$19.95
00672448	Miles Davis – Originals, Vol. 1	$19.95
00672451	Miles Davis – Originals, Vol. 2	$19.95
00672450	Miles Davis – Standards, Vol. 1	$19.95
00672449	Miles Davis – Standards, Vol. 2	$19.95
00672479	Dizzy Gillespie Collection	$19.95
00673214	Freddie Hubbard	$14.95
00672382	Tom Harrell – Jazz Trumpet	$19.95
00672363	Jazz Trumpet Solos	$9.95
00672506	Chuck Mangione Collection	$19.95
00672525	Arturo Sandoval – Trumpet Evolution	$19.95

MORE PUBLICATIONS FEATURING
OSCAR PETERSON

OSCAR PETERSON

PG Music Inc.

In this breakthrough CD-ROM, Peterson takes you on an exciting musical journey through his life and career, integrating interactive audio/visual performances with on-screen piano display and notation. There is a full range of playback features to slow the tempo, step through each piece note by note, loop, or transpose to your favorite key. Includes 14 performances by Peterson (The Smudge • City Lights • Hogtown Blues • Place St-Henri • Blues for Scoti • and more), 10 MIDI transcriptions of his famous blues performances, live video and audio commentary, an interactive autobiography, a complete discography, a time line, a photo gallery, a helpful user's guide, and much more!

00451047 CD-ROM $79.95

OSCAR PETERSON –
THE CLASSIC TRIOS

Keyboard Signature Licks

Learn how to play piano in the style of Oscar Peterson! Analyzes 14 of his trademark pieces: C-Jam Blues • Cheek to Cheek • Come Rain or Come Shine • Do Nothin' Till You Hear from Me • Don't Get Around Much Anymore • The Girl from Ipanema • I Got It Bad and That Ain't Good • The Lady Is a Tramp • My One and Only Love • Quiet Nights of Quiet Stars • Take the "A" Train • That Old Black Magic • and more.

00695871 Book/CD Pack $22.95

OSCAR PETERSON – JAZZ EXERCISES,
MINUETS, ETUDES & PIECES FOR PIANO

Legendary jazz pianist Oscar Peterson has long been devoted to the education of piano students. In this book he offers dozens of pieces designed to empower the student, whether novice or classically trained, with the technique needed to become an accomplished jazz pianist.

00311225 ....$9.95

OSCAR PETERSON – JAZZ PIANO SOLOS

Includes 8 Peterson classics for jazz piano: The Continental • Gravy Waltz • Hallelujah Time • Hymn to Freedom • Roundalay • Smedley's Blues • The Smudge • The Strut.

00672542 Piano Transcriptions.............................$14.95

OSCAR PETERSON –
MUSIC IN THE KEY OF OSCAR

with Ella Fitzgerald, Dizzy Gillespie, Quincy Jones, Norman Granz and more

VIEW Video

Oscar Peterson: Music in the Key of Oscar is a music documentary that traces the history of this piano legend from his early days as Montreal's teenage boogie-woogie sensation through his rise to international celebrity. Highlights include: Caravan • Tenderly • Nigerian Marketplace • and more!

00320560 DVD..$24.95

OSCAR PETERSON

PG Music Inc.

This fabulous book/CD pack features transcriptions of 18 piano solos by the legendary Oscar Peterson, taken directly from the original recordings. The solos are divided into two groups: eight (Chicago Blues • Hymn to Freedom • Nightingale • Night Time • and more) and ten selections in *Oscar Peterson Plays the Blues* (Blues Etude • Greasy Blues • Oscar's Boogie • R.B. Blues • Ron's Blues • and more). Includes an intro by the editor complete with performance notes, a welcome letter from Oscar Peterson and great photos, with Oscar's captions, throughout. The CD contains performances of each transcription played by gifted jazz pianist Miles Black.

00294030 Book/CD Pack $39.95

OSCAR PETERSON ORIGINALS

Transcriptions, Lead Sheets and Performance Notes

5 original Peterson compositions transcribed for piano: The Cakewalk • The Gentle Waltz • He Has Gone • Love Ballade • Sushi.

00672544 Piano Transcriptions..............................$9.95

OSCAR PETERSON PLAYS BROADWAY

18 songs arranged for piano: All the Things You Are • Baubles, Bangles and Beads • Body and Soul • Come Rain or Come Shine • Easter Parade • If I Were a Bell • Just in Time • The Lady Is a Tramp • Maria • On a Clear Day • People • Strike up the Band • Summertime • The Surrey with the Fringe on Top • There's a Small Hotel • 'Til Tomorrow • Who Can I Turn To • Wouldn't It Be Lovely.

00672532 Piano Transcriptions..............................$19.95

OSCAR PETERSON PLAYS DUKE ELLINGTON

17 transcriptions of one of the greatest piano players of our time performing the works of one of the greatest composers of our time. Includes: Band Call • C-Jam Blues • Caravan • Cotton Tail • Do Nothin' Till You Hear from Me • Don't Get Around Much Anymore • I Got It Bad and That Ain't Good • In a Mellow Tone • John Hardy's Wife • Just a Settin' and a Rockin' • Night Train • Prelude to a Kiss • Rockin' in Rhythm • Satin Doll • Sophisticated Lady • Take the "A" Train • Things Ain't What They Used to Be.

00672531 Piano Transcriptions.............................$19.95

OSCAR PETERSON TRIO – CANADIANA SUITE

In 1964 Oscar Peterson wrote a collection of compositions inspired by towns and regions in his native Canada. The resulting *Canadiana Suite* includes: Ballad to the East • Blues of the Prairies • Hogtown Blues • Land of the Misty Giants • Laurentide Waltz • March Past • Place St. Henri • Wheatland.

00672543 Piano Transcriptions...............................$7.95

OSCAR PETERSON TRIOS

19 authentic transcriptions, including: Blues Etude • Hymn to Freedom • Misty • Quiet Nights of Quiet Stars • Witchcraft • and more.

00672533 Piano Transcriptions.............................$24.95

THE VERY BEST OF OSCAR PETERSON

18 transcriptions from one of the greatest and most revered jazz pianists, including: A Child Is Born • The Continental • Gravy Waltz • I'm Old Fashioned • It Ain't Necessarily So • Little Girl Blue • Love Is Here to Stay • Moanin' • My One and Only Love • Noreen's Nocturne • On the Trail • Over the Rainbow • Place St. Henri • Rockin' Chair • 'Round Midnight • Stella by Starlight • Sweet Georgia Brown • That's All.

00672534 Piano Transcriptions.............................$19.95

For More Information, See Your Local Music Dealer, Or Write To:

HAL•LEONARD®
C O R P O R A T I O N
7777 W. Bluemound Rd. P.O. Box 13819 Milwaukee, WI 53213

Visit Hal Leonard Online at
www.halleonard.com

Prices, contents and availability subject to change without notice.